What people are saying about Huntington Woods Elementary School

"This is a shining light in Michigan and in the nation of what we want education to be."

--Robert Schiller, former Michigan Superintendent of Schools

"My daughter has been given that wonderful gift of a love for learning and excitement for school from the wonderfully dedicated teachers, the most extraordinary, gifted principal around, and what I think is the most important-- the philosophy that intertwines all of them."

--Kathy Van Essen, parent of a Huntington Woods student

"This is a great school that puts the needs of the students first."

--Visitor to Huntington Woods

"Before coming to Huntington Woods in the third grade, our son was often depressed and struggling to keep on task at school. He had lost most of his enthusiasm for learning...In the environment that Huntington Woods offers, he was able to work within a group of children on his individual needs. In areas where he excelled, there was no limit as to what he could learn, and in areas that were difficult, there was no judgment or category that he was put into. Thank you for believing that energetic children need space, movement, a variety of levels, hands-on activities, and choices...What you do works. Our son leaves Huntington with high levels of achievement, confidence, and self-esteem."

--Judy Omlor-Sobesky, parent

"I like the cooperative atmosphere at this school. I've been impressed by the enthusiasm my son has shown toward his work and toward school. He wants to learn and is having fun doing it."

--Parent of a third grade student

"Those that are lucky enough to spend their elementary years with you will develop socially, emotionally, and intellectually into the types of individuals we want and need to lead us in the future."

--Eric Vermeulen, Principal of Cooper Elementary School, Kalamazoo, Michigan

"Thank you for the care and concern that you exhibit as you interact with each child. The students are learning communication, cooperation, consideration and conservation life skills that will prove invaluable in the coming years. The spark of knowledge has been carefully tended in *every* student to allow him or her to reach full potential, a rare idea in today's public school setting! ...Keep watching...Huntington Woods alumni will accomplish great things in the future."

-- Parent Scheryl Van Den Berg

"We were impressed by the cordial, respectful treatment of students by teachers, and *vice versa.*"

--Visitor

"...In public education since 1961, I believe I know what to look for in a school building to determine if good teaching and learning are taking place. Huntington Woods is the very best!

This is what I observed. I saw students who lead; I saw independence in learning taking place; I saw youngsters who are confident and self-assured; I saw "family" being practiced. And why not — I saw the same attributes and behaviors in the adults. Your commitment to choice theory and reality therapy is so readily apparent. I now know why Dr. Glasser refers to your school so frequently when he is citing examples of schools that practice the concepts that underpin his philosophy regarding relationships and schools.

Thank you for having the vision and the courage to lead the way."

--Ted Morris, Superintendent, Fennville Public Schools

"One girl explained to me how different it was at Huntington Woods. Her old school teacher was always writing names on the board for the slightest mistakes and then taking away recesses. 'That never happens here,' she said. I asked which school had the best-behaved students and she said, 'Here, because we don't get punished.'

I hope [people] will be able to pick up on the self-assessment, the self-control, and the conflict resolution that are being taught--the inner changes are the ones that last.

--Hank Benjamin, an elementary educator

Quality Is the Key

Last month my friend and I hosted all the visitors. At the very end, everybody was asking us to sign their books because they thought that we had done a really good job.

And one lady asked us if we could give her some words of wisdom, because we are at a Quality School. I wrote, 'Quality is the key.'

--Carrie, a fifth-grade student

Quality Is the Key

Stories from
Huntington Woods School

Sally A. Ludwig, M.A.
and
Kaye W. Mentley, M.A.

KWM Educational Services, Inc.

QUALITY IS THE KEY: Stories from Huntington Woods School. Copyright © 1997 by Sally A. Ludwig and Kaye W. Mentley. All rights reserved.
Published by KWM Educational Services, Inc., 4967 Chableau Drive, Wyoming, Michigan 49509. Fax 616-534-1457.

Photographs by Connie Baker
Cover design by Jack Sprat Design

The stories in this book are all true to the spirit of Huntington Woods School. Almost all of them describe things that actually happened; one or two represent composites of students or conversations. Some names in the text have been changed to protect the privacy of students and their families.

Library of Congress book number 97-92693

ISBN: 0-9660916-0-4

Printed in the United States of America.

To two wise and caring individuals:

Our father, Dr. Robert Ludwig;
he is our greatest model of lifelong learning, loving, and living,

and

Dr. William Glasser, our mentor and friend,
who dreamed of Quality Schools so that we might bring
the dream to life.

Contents

Foreword by William Glasser, M.D.   *xv*

Chapter 1   Welcome to Huntington Woods Elementary School   1

     Claire: One student's story   3
     A school designed for quality   6
     What is a Quality School?   9

Chapter 2   Philosophy of a Quality School   15

     Choice Theory: Why people behave as they do   18
     Reality Therapy: Making a plan to improve things   27

Chapter 3   Designing a Student-Centered Environment   33

     Meeting the need for belonging   40
     Meeting the need for power and worth   44
     Meeting the need for freedom   48
     Meeting the need for fun   52

Chapter 4   **Multi-Age Learning Families**   57

    Family meetings   64
    Accelerated learning   69
    Students with special needs   73
    Team teaching   82

Chapter 5 **Lead Management**   91

    Role of the principal   97
    Decision-making   101
    Collaborative planning and professional development   102
    Lead management in the classroom   109

Chapter 6 **Self-Evaluation**   125

    Evaluation for students   127
    Evaluation for adults   144
    Evaluation for the school   151

Chapter 7 **Quality Learning**   159

    Homework   163
    Learning Family Play   167
    Community Service as Useful Learning: Casey's Restaurant 171
    Teaching Reading   174
    Using Technology instead of Textbooks   184
    Learning Choice Theory   188

Chapter 8 **Parental Involvement**   197

    Family Council   204

Conclusion   211

References and Resources   215
Acknowledgements   223

Foreword

During the many years I have worked in schools, I began to develop the picture of the kind of elementary school I would like my children to attend. In the 1960's that school was a School Without Failure, and one came into being in Palo Alto, California. The principal was Donald O'Donnell and it was a joy to be in that school. Time passed and that school disappeared, but I kept working, now for my grandchildren, as my children were grown. Then in the late 1980's, armed with Choice Theory and the quality ideas of W. Edwards Deming, I began to picture a school without failure that had progressed to a Quality School.

Joining me in seeing that new picture was a visionary, charismatic principal, Kaye Mentley, who led an elementary school in Wyoming, Michigan. By 1992 that school was beginning to move but progress was slow; too many teachers were not on board with the ideas. Then Kaye was given a new school and told to staff it with teachers who shared our vision, and things took off. That school is now Huntington Woods. It is too late for my children but I still have grandchildren it could affect. It is now a working model of a Quality School.

As you read this book you will see what can be done with powerful ideas by dedicated teachers who have become Specialists in Quality School teaching. What they do is as different from what traditional teachers do as a medical specialty such as surgery is different from general practice in medicine. Think of your children and grandchildren and how much they could benefit by getting started in a school like this.

There is nothing going on here that could not go on in your neighborhood school. It costs no more and, with no discipline problems, possibly less. But more than money is needed if we are going to change our schools. It is ideas and public interest in these ideas. It is people like you and your neighbors. After you read this book, get a group of interested young parents together and read it with them. Their children need a Quality School. Encourage them to get groups together and do the same. If we are to have a Huntington Woods in your neighborhood, this book is the tool that could get the process started. Use it; don't let it languish on your shelves.

William Glasser, M.D., President of the William Glasser Institute

Chapter 1

WELCOME TO HUNTINGTON WOODS ELEMENTARY SCHOOL

Claire: One Student's Story
A School Designed for Quality
The Conditions for Quality

Chapter 1

Welcome to Huntington Woods Elementary School

Since Kimberly started coming here to school, she is like a new child. After having lost her when she attended her first school, we have our happy daughter back again.

--Parent of a Huntington Woods student

Claire: One Student's Story

What can a school do to help an intelligent child who faces serious challenges in life? Eight-year-old Claire had been in a residential program for severely emotionally impaired children at a local mental health care facility. School principal Kaye Mentley tells that, upon her discharge, Claire's parents wanted to enroll her at Huntington Woods Elementary School.

Claire's symptoms were fairly classic for a diagnosis of severe emotional impairment--lying, stealing, foul language, physical aggression. Her discharge recommendation called for a full-time placement in a room for severely emotionally impaired children, with a maximum of nine other children, a full-time teacher, of course, a full-time instructional paraprofessional assigned to her, separate music class, separate recess, separate lunch from the rest of the students, an adult with her any time she was out of the classroom. And she was to see a school social worker twice a week. I said to Claire's mother, 'You have to understand that if you enroll her here, she's not going to get any of that.' She said, 'Yes, I understand. But we want to try it.' So we agreed.

Two years after Claire came to Huntington Woods, Kaye Mentley was in the hallway one day talking with teachers visiting the school when Claire, now a fifth-grade student, came along the hall. Mrs. Mentley called her over and said,

Claire, I know this is short notice, but since you are going to speak at the conference next week, would you talk with these visitors? What are you going to tell people at the conference when they ask about your experience at our school?

Claire replied,

Well, I'm going to tell them that I came here and I have completely turned around. I used to be in, like, a mental hospital. I used to lie, and steal. I was very mouthy. I don't do that anymore. Mrs. Mentley knows that I can still act like a brat at times, but I'm working on that. I have goals in my life now and I'm not going to be like that.

One of the visiting teachers asked, "Have you changed as a person since you've been here?"

Yes, Claire answered. This school helped me change my whole life. Before, at my other schools, I was a horrible student. I was always getting mad, and when I got mad I would steal and lie. I didn't get much attention, so I felt like if I stole then maybe I'd get a little attention. All they gave me was a time out or a grounding, or even a detention or a suspension. So I went through counseling at school, but that didn't help. The schoolwork we did was really boring because I'd do the same work over and over again. I used to have to do stuff in third grade that I did in first. I didn't like it and neither did my mom.

And then when I came here--the teachers and the students here helped me so I wouldn't do those things. I got more attention and I told myself I didn't have to do it anymore, getting in trouble. If I got grouchy, my teachers told me to calm down, work the problem out, don't fight, just solve it by talking. And that really helped me a lot. It's been two and a half years since I've done the things I used to do. They helped me, and now I can evaluate my behavior and figure out how to do better. I'm doing great here. I wish this school went through college!

Claire's home life is still very difficult, but she is happy and successful, especially at school. A visitor who knew of her history could not pick her out among the students in her learning family. Now, she has made many friends, and loves to go into the preschoolers' room to help the teacher with the young children. She is one of our student leaders, and is a student host, speaking to adult audiences. She has mastered all of her grade level standards and is working on those for sixth and seventh grades. One of Claire's teachers, Sandy Hartman, said:

Claire is another child we have seen absolutely blossom here. Within the first few months after she came to Huntington Woods, most of the behaviors that had previously been labeled as severe emotional impairment disappeared. Some old learned behaviors might creep in once in awhile, but she, the child who wasn't helpful and wanted nothing to do with anyone, and was street wise and knew it all--real tough--has grown tremendously. She is helpful now, and loves to help with little ones. She is a wonderful writer, and is able to express a lot of her feelings in writing. Now she is speaking for Huntington Woods, going to make public presentations with teachers and with Kaye, and talking with visitors. Her power is coming in a positive way, and she knows she does not need that other kind of power. She doesn't need to do the things she did before to meet her needs. It has been fun, and fascinating, watching that change.

What does it take for a child to change direction as Claire has? At Huntington Woods School, we believe that every child can achieve quality learning and gain effective control of his or her life in an environment that provides the right conditions. In a Quality School, the entire system is designed to help all its students improve their lives through learning--learning the information, skills, and values that will help them live successfully and responsibly, now and in the future. Our goal is to help students to achieve their highest potential and develop personal responsibility and self-control, not by coercion, threats, or rewards, but by teaching them to fulfill their basic human needs in responsible, effective ways, and to solve problems by talking them through.

The mission statement of Huntington Woods, **learning will add quality to each student's life**, is being lived in this school every day. The teachers and staff have designed every aspect of our system to make educational experiences valuable, enjoyable, and satisfying for everyone involved--students, teachers, parents, administrators and support staff. This book will tell about some examples of what is being done and, by explaining the thinking behind our decisions, why it is working.

A School Designed for Quality

Huntington Woods Elementary School is part of the Wyoming Public School District of Wyoming, Michigan. When increased enrollment led district administrators to begin planning for a new elementary school, they recognized a unique opportunity to offer a very different choice to parents and students. They gathered interested administrators, teachers, and Principal Kaye Mentley, and established a "dream team" whose mandate was to envision a plan for the new school. With this unusual opportunity to make a fresh start, our team adopted a mental "clean slate" approach, and decided there were several new initiatives that we wanted to have at our school.

We have chosen Dr. William Glasser's work in **Quality Schools, Choice Theory** and **Reality Therapy** as our philosophical base. We believe that this gives us our best opportunity to have students do real quality learning in school. Everyone working at Huntington Woods, teachers, principal, and support staff, has decided to support it completely. Chapter 2, The Philosophy of a Quality School, summarizes Choice Theory and Reality Therapy and introduces ways that they can be applied in the school setting.

An important difference in our school is our design orientation. Decisions about structure, scheduling and calendar, instructional planning and practices, discipline, and every other area are made to best serve students' best interests. Our students and their parents are our "customers," and we emphasize service to them by designing a school that furthers the intellectual, academic, social, and personal growth of children, and the well being of families. Chapter 3, Designing a Student-Centered Environment, gives examples of design features at Huntington Woods that create a need-satisfying setting for learning.

We wanted our students in inclusive multi-age learning families, each family with a team of teachers. Chapter 4, about the learning families, discusses the class meetings each one uses daily, the provisions for accelerating learning, teaching children with special needs, and team teaching.

Our management system, presented in Chapter 5, is designed to eliminate coercion from our environment. By leaving behind the traditional system of reward and punishment, which is detrimental to people's intrinsic motivation, we enhance the conditions for quality achievement by children and adults. The role of the principal as the primary leader, facilitator, and model is described. This section also describes the collaborative planning and professional growth time that we have built into our regular weekly schedule, and shows some of the ways we use lead management in the classroom.

Self-evaluation is a vital part of improving one's performance. As introduced in the following sections and further discussed in Chapter 6, we teach students this practice and use it together with concurrent evaluation where appropriate. Staff members set professional goals and evaluate their own work, and we also evaluate the larger systems of the school to continually improve it.

To create the quality learning opportunities we want for our students (see the conditions for quality below, and Chapter 7), teachers plan thematic lessons that demonstrate the relationships among all subject areas. They use interesting projects to teach the curriculum in a context of relevant, useful work. Students learn cooperatively much of the time, developing skills that will serve them well in adolescence and adulthood. Another difference at Huntington is that we do not use textbooks. Instead of having students plodding through a textbook page after page, we make use of technology and hands-on learning. Students and adults learn Choice Theory and Reality Therapy, and find them eminently useful in daily life as well as in school.

Extensive parent involvement is important to our success, and we do a lot to encourage parents to participate in their children's education. See Chapter 8 for information about parents and the school.

In keeping with the emphasis on constant improvement toward quality, the systems we have designed are continually being evaluated and improved. We have found that the more we can give students what they need and what they want, and make their school a welcoming place where they feel a sense of belonging and importance, the better students behave, the more enthusiastic they are about learning, and the better they succeed.

What is a Quality School?

A Quality School is one in which students discover that learning adds *value*--usefulness and meaning--to their lives. The originator of this concept, William Glasser, has said (1997) that to judge itself to be a quality school, a school should have these characteristics:

- The school is free of discipline problems as a major concern-- incidents will occur, but there are no serious ongoing problems with discipline.
- Achievement scores on state assessments are at the seventy-fifth percentile or above.
- In all subjects, all students achieve competence that they can demonstrate or explain. All grades below competence (or what is now a B) will be eliminated, which means that the only records kept will be of competent learning. To get credit, students will demonstrate competence to the teacher or a designated teacher assistant.
- "Schooling" (rote learning of material divorced from relevance to students' lives) is replaced by useful education.
- Beyond competency, all students do some work each year that both they and their teachers consider quality work. This is work significantly beyond competence. It will receive an 'A' grade or higher, and give hard-working students a chance to show that they can excel.
- Students and adults know Choice Theory to a depth appropriate to their comprehension. They understand the concepts and how to use them in their lives and in their work in school. Parents will be encouraged to participate in study groups led by teachers or by parent volunteers to become familiar with the book *Choice Theory, A New Psychology of Personal Freedom* (Glasser, forthcoming in 1997).
- The school is a joyful place, and those working in it--students *and* adults--find satisfaction in their work. Following Dr. W. Edwards Deming (1986), we believe that quality education is a joyful process.

The Huntington Woods family believes:

School should be need fulfilling for students, staff and parents. All people have needs for survival, belonging, power, freedom and fun.

People learn best through cooperation rather than competition, by working together, with each individual learning at his or her own pace.

All students can learn and be successful when teachers are lead managers, rather than boss managers. Quality flourishes in an environment free of coercion.

All problems will be solved by talking them through, without anyone threatening or hurting anyone else.

Self-evaluation leads to quality performances and learning experiences.

QUALITY
- is the best we can achieve at a particular time.
- can constantly be improved.
- is always useful, never destructive. What students learn should be useful and meaningful.
- always feels good. The higher the quality, the longer the good feeling lasts.

A Quality School is always in the process of growing and improving. The self-designation of quality does not mean a school has achieved perfection, but that the process is well established and ongoing. Quality is built through the cooperation and collaboration of all who are involved in the school, administrators, teachers, support staff, students and parents. Just as all members of the school community must be willing participants, all share in its success.

In keeping with the third condition for quality (see below), a Quality School is not certified by the William Glasser Institute or by any other body outside of the school. Rather, people at the school evaluate themselves and how well their school is meeting all of the conditions for quality. They judge whether their organization is a Quality School and when it achieves this status.

Once students experience the satisfaction of being involved in high-quality learning, they will not be content doing just enough to get by. It takes hard work to do one's best, but our teachers know how to make learning useful, interesting and fun. Students become willing to exert the effort to learn and work to the level of quality when they realize that their lives are better because of it. Through an understanding of Choice Theory, teachers and administrators recognize that we cannot *make* students achieve quality learning, but we can create the conditions for it. These conditions are:

- a warm, caring environment free of coercion
- useful learning: the things students are asked to learn are important and will help them
- self-evaluation, in which teachers and students at Huntington Woods assess the quality of their own work and decide how to improve it.

A Quality School meets these *conditions for quality*:

- **A supportive environment of warm, caring relationships, free of coercion**

People work and learn best in an environment in which they can satisfy their basic psychological needs for belonging, power, freedom and fun. To get this, we put the emphasis on building strong relationships in which students trust teachers and believe the adults in school are working for their best interests. We want adult staff members to know each other well and support each other as professional colleagues and friends. Such a climate encourages everyone to do his or her best, most creative work.

A key to creating trusting relationships is to eliminate coercion, which is the idea that teachers can and should compel students to learn and to behave in desirable ways, and that a principal's job is to "boss" teachers. Coercion, because it makes students and teachers adversaries instead of friends, is the enemy of quality learning, and coercive management also destroys the motivation for adults to do their highest quality work. To eliminate it, we get rid of all threats, rewards, punishments, ridicule, lowering of grades and anything else that could be construed as forcing a student or teacher to do what he or she does not want to do. Our role as educational leaders is to move from boss managing to *lead managing*, in which people choose to follow a leader because they believe this person has their benefit in mind, as well as success in the task at hand.

One of the chief ways we create a coercion-free environment is our commitment to the belief that **all problems will be solved by talking them through, without anyone hurting or threatening anyone else.** Even the youngest children understand this. We have adopted the use of *Reality Therapy*, a counseling technique developed by William Glasser, which provides a method that can be learned and used by everyone for talking through problems.

- **Learning which is meaningful, relevant and useful to students**

Quality is always useful; teachers present material to students that they can easily recognize as relevant to their lives. We focus our teaching on skills that are important to a successful life, emphasizing speaking, reading, writing, mathematical calculation, scientific investigation and a lot of problem solving. Students work on these skills in all classes so that well before graduation they are able to read, speak, write and calculate in a way that they and their teachers agree is quality.

One important way we teach is by allowing students to apply useful skills in real-life situations. Hands-on experience convinces students that learning is useful and fun, and shows them that usefulness includes enjoyment, meaning and aesthetic value as well as practical utility. Also, students are encouraged to contribute to the usefulness of what is being done. Teachers ask students for their ideas about what they want to learn, how they would like to study the things they need to learn, and how the classroom should be run to make it a good learning environment for everyone.

Quality is never destructive. This is one of the reasons we emphasize cooperation and collaboration over competition (where someone must be the loser).

- **Self-evaluation for everyone**

Self-evaluation is the difficult skill of looking at what we have done and deciding how to make it better. In life, we can self-evaluate almost everything that we do, from work on a project to our interaction with another person in a particular situation. As we learn to make improvements based on our self-evaluations, each thing we attempt goes better.

We teach self-evaluation directly and also by example, as all our employees continually evaluate their own performance. Because Huntington Woods is founded on innovation and improvement, we ask ourselves questions such as, "Is this the best we can offer our students? How could I make this experience better?" We are not in the business of establishing tradition and continuing to do things because we have always done them. We *are* in the business of constant evaluation and improvement. Our school continues to evolve as staff members evaluate how well aspects of it are working and make changes for the better.

Students are taught to evaluate their own work and behavior honestly. Beginning at the kindergarten level, they learn to look carefully at what they do and ask themselves, "Is this my best work? How could I improve it?" and also, "Is my behavior working to get me what I want? What could I do differently that would work better?" As long as students want to work to improve the quality of what they do, they will always receive credit for it, and any grade can be raised. For example, in May two first-grade boys re-took spelling tests that they had originally taken the previous October. Although they had passed the tests in the fall, the boys thought they could do better. And they did! Students are encouraged to keep improving their work until it reaches a level that they and their teachers agree is cause for pride.

In this way, they learn that imperfections in their work are not marks of failure, but valuable opportunities to learn to do better.

We have had parents tell us that through the skill of self-evaluation they have seen real academic growth in their children.

Chapter 2

PHILOSOPHY OF A QUALITY SCHOOL

Choice Theory: Why People Behave as they Do
Reality Therapy: Making a Plan to Improve Things

Chapter 2

Philosophy of a Quality School

What really motivates people to learn, cooperate, or do anything else? How can an understanding of human psychology help us teach students effectively? An understanding of Choice Theory and Reality Therapy is fundamental to our approach at Huntington Woods. These form the psychological framework for quality, which gives us a solid base for consistent goal setting and helps us develop clear communication. All our staff members and students, and many of the parents, learn these concepts and practice applying them.

Choice Theory: Why People Behave as they Do

Choice Theory is a new explanation of human behavior that emphasizes the fact that we each choose all that we do, for reasons that are inside us. We cannot be controlled from the outside by promises of reward or threats of punishment, and we are all responsible for the choices we make. This biological and psychological model was developed by psychiatrist and educator William Glasser, M.D., who realized that the most common theory, the cause-and-effect model which he designates as external control psychology (Glasser 1997), does not adequately explain how people are motivated or why they act as they do.

External control psychology is based on the idea that people are *externally motivated* by events outside of us; an event in the environment causes a response in the organism. For example, most people believe that they do not choose their behaviors, especially in the sense that they do not choose how they feel emotionally or how their bodies function. They believe that what they do and feel and what goes on in their bodies are natural, inevitable reactions to stimuli, the things that happen outside of them (Glasser 1989). This belief is reflected in our language by such phrases as "he really makes me angry" or "I was in a hurry, but I had to stop at a red light."

According to this external control model, teachers can motivate students by rewarding desired behavior and punishing misbehavior: further, it is right, and even their moral duty, to try to control students. In contrast, Choice Theory teaches that people are *intrinsically motivated*. It asserts that because we choose our own behavior, we control ourselves. No one can control another person's behavior. In fact, trying to make people do something that they do not want to do weakens our relationship with them, and they become less likely to choose to do what we want them to.

For example, William Glasser writes (1990), most people believe that students stop talking because the teacher asks for silence or that jail sentences deter crime. But [Choice] theory points out that this is not the case. Students keep quiet only when they believe it is to their benefit to do as the teacher asks; otherwise they keep talking. And our jails are filled with lawbreakers who have been there before and have not been deterred by that experience.

It is always what we want at the time that causes our behavior. The outside event (stimulus) may seem to be the cause, but it never is...teachers tell students every day to work hard; even though they are punished, many students still do not work hard. In fact, many do even less after they are punished. The same goes for reward: It is not the reward but the person's evaluation of how much he or she wants the reward that determines behavior.

What happens outside of us has a lot to do with what we choose to do, but the outside event does not cause our behavior. What we get, and all we ever get from the outside is information; how we choose to act on this information is up to us. Therefore, the information that the students get from the teacher, which includes how this information is given, is very important...But the students are the ones who make the ultimate judgment about how important it is to them. The more important they think it is, the more they will do what they are asked and the better they will do it.   (Pages 39, 40-41)

He explains further with another example:

When the phone rings, I pick it up and talk for a moment, then hang it up. Then let's say I ask you, "Why did I pick up the phone?" Most people would say, "You picked it up because it rang." It seems like common sense. The ringing was the stimulus, and picking it up was the appropriate behavior for that stimulus. People don't usually pick up phones that are not ringing. So people believe that the cause of my picking up the phone was the ringing.

[Choice] Theory says, "No, you did not pick up the phone because it rang. No one has ever picked up a phone because it rang. All of your behavior comes from inside yourself." In my own family, I have an example. We have a child, and she is a very good child in many respects, but she does not answer the phone. We know she is not deaf--she hears fine--and we would ask her, "Why don't you answer the phone?" and she would say, "I don't do phone." This is not a baby girl we are talking about; she is forty-one years old.

The ring of the phone does not *make* you do anything. All behavior (everything we do from birth until death) is chosen. Some sneezes or stomach rumblings, things like that are not chosen, but *any behavior that has any discernible psychological purpose is chosen.* When you answer the phone, you are choosing to do it. The ring of the phone is part of the operation, but not the cause of the operation. The cause of all of our behavior is inside of our heads. You have a picture in your head of talking to a person who is calling, and you want that to become reality, so you answer the phone.

We believe that perhaps one of the greatest things a school can do for its students is to teach them that 'You are in control of your own behavior. You are the one who is doing the choosing, and you can choose behavior that will be effective in getting what you want and making your life what you want it to be.

The main ideas of Choice Theory are:
- behavior is chosen and purposeful,
- the basic needs,
- the pictures in our heads, and
- the concept of total behavior.

Once we understand these, we can use our understanding to make better choices and improve our lives.

- **The purpose of behavior: Meeting basic needs**

Everything people and other living creatures do has a purpose; we choose all of our behaviors to try to satisfy powerful inborn needs. These needs are coded into human genetic structure as instructions for living our lives, and are just as much a part of our genetic heritage as the color of our eyes.

The basic needs shared by all human beings are:

- *survival*

  The need to survive is met by having air to breathe, water and food, rest, shelter, safety and opportunity to reproduce. A person with a very strong need to survive is likely to be concerned with security, take few risks, and view new ideas and unfamiliar people with distrust. In the school setting, hungry children must be nourished before they will pay attention to schoolwork, as teachers know. Another aspect of the need to survive that is important in school is physical and psychological safety.

- *belonging*

  We fulfill the need to belong through affection and love, sharing, affiliations, and cooperating, which build feelings of connection. In a Quality School, strong, caring relationships are the cornerstone of the learning environment. William Glasser writes (1986, page 22), addressing teachers, that

  Many a lonely student works hard and learns to live a successful life because he encounters a warm and caring teacher. Even though his need to belong may be totally unsatisfied outside of school, if he has you as a good friend, he may consider himself reasonably satisfied...a good school or even a good teacher can do much to overcome an inadequate home.

- *power*

  This means the need for a sense of worth and the respect of others, and having a meaningful impact on the world. One way we fulfill the need for power is through being listened to by someone who matters to us; other ways include achievement, gaining new knowledge and abilities, success and recognition, and gaining a sense of self-control.

- *freedom*
  We fulfill the need for freedom by making choices. It can be difficult for a child in school to meet this need, and when students go through their school days being told what to do, when, and with whom, they may seek more freedom by choosing to resist direction or ignore lessons.

- *fun*
  We can satisfy our need for fun with play or any activity that gets us to laugh. Fun is directly allied with learning; play is the way we learn much of what we need to know to live. The close connection between fun and learning means that dullness and boredom are obstacles to effective learning, while enjoyment and laughter enhance it. Exercising creativity is among the most pleasurable of human experiences; the enjoyment that comes with creating is probably the genetic incentive for flexibility to reorganize our thinking and other behavior, which has been so important to human survival.

Chapter 3, Creating a Student-centered Environment, gives examples of how opportunities for needs-satisfaction are built into the Huntington Woods system.

Basic needs are closely linked to how we feel. When the behavior we choose succeeds in meeting a basic need, we feel very good. For example, when we are hungry we know that it will feel very good to eat a tasty meal; when we feel powerless, we know that it will feel good if we can get someone to listen to us. If our attempt to meet a need fails, we feel pain. From these feelings, we begin as small children to learn particular behaviors that fulfill our needs.

- **Quality world pictures: The core of our lives**

Our behaviors have the ultimate purpose of meeting basic needs, but we go about this indirectly. For example, if I try to meet my need for power, I usually do not tell myself, "I'm going to get some power." Instead, I might work to finish a task, or do my exercise workout. I have an image in my mind of myself completing the task, for example, and the pleasant feeling of satisfaction I know my accomplishment will bring. This mental image is one of my *quality world pictures*.

As we grow and learn new behaviors, we accumulate memories of experiences in which, because our basic needs are being satisfied, we feel the best. We keep images of the people, things and behaviors associated with these good feelings in our memories, and build ideas based on them of how we can satisfy our needs. This set of perceptual pictures becomes our *quality world*, our ideas of the world as we would like it to be. It includes pictures of ourselves as the people we hope to be. Quality world pictures are highly individual because, although people share the same basic needs, the need-satisfying experiences we have are unique to each of us.

The quality world is the most important part of an individual's life, because each person pursues the pictures in it to try to satisfy needs. We only pay close attention to perceptual pictures that we have placed in our quality worlds; we care strongly about those, and willingly work hard to get them to become reality. Students put pictures of teachers, school and learning into their quality worlds when their experiences in school bring them the good feelings of fulfilled needs. Our efforts to create a need-satisfying environment at our school are directed toward this goal.

- **The urge to behave: A question of imbalance**

To enable us to satisfy basic needs, our perceptual systems are always busy comparing what is actually happening with a quality world perception of what we want to happen. The more alike the two are, then the more in control we feel; whatever we are doing is successfully getting us what we want, so we continue to do it. When there is a discrepancy between a quality world picture and our perceptions of events in the real world, then we feel an urge to behave. We do, feel, and/or think something different, trying to change the situation to make it more like our picture of what we want. William Glasser uses the analogy of balance scales to symbolize these comparisons: on one pan of the scale is a perceptual picture of what we want; on the other is our perception of what we have. When the two match, the scales are evenly balanced. When there is a mismatch, and the two pans of our scales are out of balance, then we feel an impulse to behave.

The following example illustrates the urge to initiate new behavior (followed by a self-evaluation):

Let's say that I, the principal, have a picture in my head of exactly what I want Huntington Woods to look like. In my picture, students and teachers have good, caring relationships with each other. That is my quality world picture, and it's very vivid and detailed. Then, when I walk down the hall at school, let's assume I see three teachers screaming at children and I see five children in the hall slugging each other. When that happens, my feelings are going to be extremely unpleasant! What I want and what I perceive are very different, and I will get a strong frustration signal, which is my urge to behave. What I might do then is yell at the students to get back to their room and be quiet, and tell the teachers I am going to write them up for that terrible scene, and so on.

That was my best attempt to try to get my picture into reality. But then the question is, How did it work for me? Will that behavior really get me closer to that picture? In this example, the answer is, No.

The behavior we choose may not be effective or even appropriate, but it is never "out of control". It is the best attempt to get what we want that we know how to make at the time. As a teacher or administrator, knowing that people's actions are their best attempt to get what they want helps me not to reject children who are, in my eyes, behaving badly. I used to think, "How could you..." and "What is the matter with you?" Now I think, "Well, that's your best attempt right now, and I think if we work together awhile, I might be able to help you see some better ways to get your needs met so you don't have to behave like that."

- **All behavior is total behavior**

Throughout our lives, everything we do is behaving, acting upon the world and ourselves (we are part of the real world) to try to get our quality world ideas to become reality. Every behavior includes:

- *doing*—for example, walking, talking
- *thinking*—worrying, remembering
- *feeling*—sad, angry
- *physiology*—headache, hands shaking.

These four components always occur at the same time, blending together to constitute a total behavior. *Feeling* is the component that we usually notice most. We almost always know what emotion we are feeling and whether it is pleasant or painful, and very seldom just feel neutral. If sometimes we cannot recognize our emotional state, then thinking about the physiological component can be a way to approach emotions. For example, if my stomach feels tense, my palms are sweating and my breathing is fast, I can identify my vague emotional sensation as fear.

Recognizing that a feeling is just one part of a total behavior helps us to learn that we can change it if we want to. The way to change a total behavior, including feelings and physiology, is to change the components we can control directly. We have the most control over what we do; we can also control our thoughts to a large extent. We have much less direct control over emotions we feel, and even less over physiological processes.

A good analogy for total behavior is to compare the aspects of behavior to the four wheels of a car. Acting and thinking are the front wheels, which we can steer; they are the components that are more accessible to our conscious control. Feeling and physiology compare to the back wheels, which follow along. Our needs are the engine that powers behavior. When I perceive a difference between a picture in my quality world of what I want to meet my needs, and what I really have at the time, that imbalance is the ignition that starts my behavior.

I always steer my car in the direction that I think will get me closer to my picture of what I want.

An example follows.

Changing total behavior

If I feel really angry with you right now, I may not be able to turn it off just like that. The emotional feeling that goes with the total behavior of angering is not something I can change directly. But what I *can* do to help myself is to stop and recognize that 'I really feel angry at Sally.' When I am feeling that, what is my body doing? Well, my heart is racing and I feel hot. What am I thinking? I think 'I want to kill her; she just makes me sick.' And what am I doing? I am pacing back and forth, clenching my fists. What is it that I want? I said that I want a great relationship with Sally. I feel angry and here is what I am thinking and doing. How is that working to get me the relationship I want? Not well at all! So I want to figure out a better behavior.

I realize that I can't simply turn off my feelings of anger. But I can think and do something different - especially 'do.' I can change my actions, even if my thoughts are more difficult to alter. So rather than pace back and forth and think that I really want to kill you, I could choose to take three deep breaths, then touch my toes four times and each time I touch my toes, think of one thing I like about you. That's just a corny off-the-cuff example. But I really could make a choice to do something like that, different from what I am doing, that would help turn my whole behavior in a more positive direction. Once I change my actions and thinking, I will feel different emotionally and physiologically. *Feelings do not need to dictate how we behave.* We are choosing our behavior, and by changing the actions and thoughts, the other components will follow - maybe not immediately, but over time the emotion and physiological state will change, too.

Reality Therapy: Making a Plan to Improve Things

> [Reality Therapy] has been proven effective in education, parenting, leadership, and management; it lends itself to any situation where people need to learn how to satisfy their needs in responsible ways...It is a flowing and adaptable communication process that allows the lead-manager principal and teacher to create a supportive environment in which individuals are freed to do quality learning.
>
> --Crawford, Bodine, Hoglund (1993, p. 44)

Dr. Glasser teaches that no matter how bad things seem, we can choose to do better with our lives, provided we are willing to make the effort to do so. Reality Therapy is the counseling approach that he developed to help individuals gain effective control over their lives by self-evaluating their behavior. Essentially a problem solving process, this is the method of talking through problems which the young student Claire credits with helping her to change. The goal of Reality Therapy is to help a person look at his or her behavior, evaluate how well that behavior is working to get his or her wants fulfilled, then figure out and put into practice better choices of behavior to meet her or his needs effectively and responsibly. (Meeting needs responsibly means satisfying them without impeding the efforts of others to meet their own needs.) Because it teaches thoughtful decision-making, and recognizes that each person is in control of and responsible for choices made, it offers a way toward lasting change.

The core question of Reality Therapy is, "Does your present behavior have a reasonable chance of getting you what you want now and will it take you in the direction you want to go?" The framework of the problem-solving process consists of these questions (as Kaye asked herself in the example of angering behavior, above):

- What do I want in this situation?
- What am I doing now?
- Is that behavior helping me or hurting me in getting what I want?
- What other behavior could I choose that would work better?

We can use this approach as self-talk to help us change what we can control so that a new, more effective total behavior can emerge. We can also use it to help someone else in a particular situation, *if* we have a good relationship with him or her. The first element of using the Reality Therapy process to counsel is to establish a warm, caring environment with genuine involvement and trust between the people involved. During their talks, the facilitator listens respectfully, allowing plenty of opportunity for the person being counseled to speak; if the tone is one of safety and support, rather than criticism, the person is more likely to accept the risk of making an honest self-evaluation and planning for change.

To have a good chance of success, a plan for new behavior should be specific, simple and achievable. The facilitator or counselor can help the person to judge how realistic it is, and only supports a plan that he or she is quite sure the client can carry out successfully. A plan should include a measurable outcome, so that a person will be able evaluate how well or poorly it has succeeded, and should identify any assistance the person believes will help them. The person guiding the process elicits a firm commitment to try the planned behavior; the commitment may be written or verbal, but should be expressed clearly by the person being counseled.

The final step in the process is to follow up by checking with the person at a later time. When counseling a student, a teacher might ask, "how do you want to let me know if your plan is working? Do you want to drop me a note, or do you want me to come and check with you?" We then make sure to talk with that child to see whether he or she needs to talk further. Students seem to appreciate the concern, which tells them that we care enough to hold them responsible for following through with the plan.

The counselor can find out whether the person tried the new behavior as planned, help him or her to evaluate how well the plan worked, discuss how it could be improved, and formulate a new plan if one is needed. As the person evaluates, the advisor can help him or her recognize and take credit for improvements achieved; successes, even if very small, help the person who tries new behavioral choices to build a *success identity*, an image in their own and others' eyes as a person who can succeed. The follow-up continues the positive support that is needed. It demonstrates that the counselor is serious about helping the person, and emphasizes a belief that the person can grow and change, even if improvement requires time and practice.

An example from the videotape *Building a Quality School* illustrates one way Reality Therapy can be used with students. One day after two girls, Tasia and Brittany, had a conflict on the playground, Kaye Mentley talked with them in her office about it:

> Kaye Mentley: Brittany and Tasia, you were sent here by your teacher because you were having a problem. Will one of you please tell me what happened?
>
> Tasia: She was calling me names, and they were really rude names.
>
> K: Where were you when this was happening?
>
> T: Out on the playground.
>
> K: What were you doing?
>
> T: I was playing with my friends, and she just came up to me and started calling me names.
>
> K: Brittany, Did you call her names?
>
> Brittany: Yes.
>
> K: Does that fit our consideration rule, for you to call her names?
>
> B: No.
>
> K: Okay. When you were calling her names when she was there playing, what did you want?
>
> B: I wanted to play with her and her friends.
>
> K: So you wanted to play with that group of girls. And what you did was--what?
>
> B: I called her names.
>
> K: Did calling her names help you get to play with her?
>
> B: No.
>
> K: All right. If you wanted to play with her again, what might help you get what you want?
>
> B: Ask.
>
> K: How would you ask her?
>
> B: Maybe go up to her and say, "Hi," and maybe say, "Can I play with you guys?"

K: Okay. Do you think that would work better than the name-calling?

B: Yeah.

K: Okay. Tasia, which do you think would work better for you?

T: If she would come up and say, "Can I please play with you?" and if we all agreed, then she could.

K: Brittany, what will happen if they say, "No, not now"? Do you have any other choices or things you might do?

B: Yeah, go and try to find some other friends.

K: Okay. What would you like to do the next time your group is outside?

B: Maybe ask if I could play with them, and if they say "No," then go play on the monkey bars or something.

K: Okay. I think your class is going outside this afternoon. When you come back in from that break, would you please come and let me know what you did, and how it worked out for you?

B: Okay.

K: All right. That would be good. Thank you, girls.

These girls' experiences every day in school have created the supportive environment necessary for such counseling. They know from all their interactions with their principal that she likes them, cares about their well-being, and will not try to coerce them, but rather tries to make school a need-satisfying place for them. Tasia and Brittany trust Mrs. Mentley and care a great deal for her; in Choice Theory terms, they have put her into their quality worlds.

Let's return to Claire's story. When Claire first started attending Huntington Woods, we told her that if she broke the school rules, we would not get angry at her, yell at her, or punish her. We would continue to treat her as a person we care about and respect, and help her learn how to make things go better. There were a few occasions during the first several weeks when she tested the rules and our commitment to doing what we had said we would do.

When she stole from another student, Kaye Mentley talked with her. She told Claire that she would not impose any punishment, that they would solve the problem by talking it through. There were, however, consequences when she stole something. "If you steal," Kaye pointed out, "the people in your learning family probably will not choose you to take care of the field trip money. You probably won't get a job working in the school store or bank." *Consequences* are events such as these that follow naturally from an action. When a penalty is imposed by someone in authority, that is a *punishment*. On another occasion, when Claire was physically aggressive toward a student on the playground, Kaye spoke with her about how, as a consequence of such behavior, the person she hit might hit her back, and other students probably would not want to be her friends.

Teachers experienced in using Reality Therapy agree that, as Jim Anderson, a specialist in school psychology writes (1995, page 39), the problem-solving approach of this technique "is oriented towards making positive changes in the present, rather than punishing students for past events." The focus is on present behaviors and solutions to problems. Punishing a student who has had problems attaining a goal is likely to damage or reinforce an already damaged self-image.

> For the student to succeed, it helps tremendously if he is able to visualize himself succeeding at his goal, and punishment may discourage this...[It] also damages the teacher-student relationship. (Page 73)

Another major component of these talks with Claire was helping her figure out how to get what she wanted in responsible ways, without hurting anyone else. As Claire learned about the basic needs and quality world pictures, she got better at identifying what she wanted in instances of problem behavior—often, attention, respect from her schoolmates, and being liked and accepted. She learned to think about what she was doing at those times. When the 'doing' part of her behavior was hitting someone, she might be feeling angry, with aroused "fight or flight" physiology, and thinking, "I'll show you that you can't ignore me". Gradually she gained the strength to make an honest self-evaluation that no, none of that behavior was getting her closer to what she wanted. Once she made this judgment, she was ready to consider other ways to behave that might help her get what she wanted more effectively, without negative consequences.

Even more importantly, Claire (and the other students, and also the adults!) can satisfy their basic needs each day because the Huntington Woods community operates in ways designed to help them do so. When, for example, a student's need for power is satisfied by having an idea for a group project accepted by the group and the teacher, he or she does not feel a need to impose power on other students by pushing them around on the playground. The next sections give some examples of ways we have developed to create an environment in which children and adults can meet their needs and be freed to achieve their quality best.

Chapter 3

DESIGNING A STUDENT-CENTERED ENVIRONMENT

Meeting the Need for Belonging
Meeting the Need for Power and Worth
Meeting the Need for Freedom
Meeting the Need for Fun

Chapter 3

DESIGNING A STUDENT-CENTERED
ENVIRONMENT

In a need-fulfilling work environment the worker's natural inclination to learn and be innovative is nurtured and preserved.
-- (Crawford, et.al. 1993)

Can you imagine seeing and hearing these things in a school?

- A student leaving school for a dental appointment at 1:30 in the afternoon who looked up at her dad and said, "I get to come back today, don't I?"
- A parent asking, "My child is getting ready for school an hour early in the morning. What are you doing?"

During her first autumn as a sixth-grade student, after moving on from Huntington Woods Elementary to middle school, Kristina wrote this composition for an assignment. Her teacher, thinking that Kristina's former teachers and principal would like to see it, sent a copy to us. Many of the innovations that help to create a high-quality environment for learning at Huntington Woods are mentioned in her essay.

My First Day Of Fifth Grade

by Kristina Brackett

I would have to say the most important day for me last year was the first day of fifth grade! It was the most important day because it was the day Huntington Woods first opened. (I had a nervous stomach that day because I didn't know what to expect at a new school.)

Huntington Woods is a one-of-a-kind school in many ways. It goes all year, but there are two-week intersessions. An intersession is where you can choose to go to school and learn about something fun or you can take off school. Huntington Woods is high in technology. They have computers, televisions, VCRs and telephones in the classrooms. Students go to the computer lab three times a week. They have multi-aged classrooms where a fifth grader can share the same class with a third grader. Huntington Woods has open classrooms. That means there are two classes with a doorway and a window in-between them. There is one class that I was in, with three classrooms together. Last year, it was the only classroom like that in the entire country.

They have lots of different things to do that other schools don't. They have a vegetable and flower garden to work on in the spring. There is also Job Corp. That is where every upper elementary child has a job to do and they do that job every day. Some jobs include: sweeping, raking, shoveling, putting up the flag, dusting, getting the trash, getting the recycling, and cleaning the playground. They also have student run businesses like a post office, a crayon factory, a chalk factory, and a bank.

At Huntington Woods we had many visitors last year. Parents, children, and teachers came to see how our school worked. Many reporters and news cameras came, also. (Some news reporters that came were from Channel 8 News and the Wyoming Advance newspaper.) Two of the most exciting groups of people that came were four teachers from Utah and movie producers from Hollywood, California that came to make a movie of our school.

So that is why the first day of fifth grade was the most important day for me last year. I had a terrific year and wouldn't change it for anything. The first day was fabulous just like the ones that followed. I wish everyone could of had a great year like mine was!

* * * * *

Huntington Woods Elementary School is founded on a student-centered design philosophy. Research into learning theory, quality management and the understanding of human behavior based on Choice Theory led our "dream team" to design the school, from classroom teaching to recess to parent involvement, to work more effectively than traditional practices. We want it to fit students better, to optimize the ways in which people think, learn and behave.

The features Kristina writes about, and the others that make Huntington Woods unique, are systemic changes. We have created a system to be need-fulfilling for students, rather than creating a system that we think will work for adults and then forcing the students to comply with it. The criterion we chose for screening all design decisions is a simple one with profound effects: what is best for the students?

Huntington Woods opened in August 1993. It is a School of Choice; all students attend because their parents apply for them to enroll. Teachers also make special application to teach here. We have approximately 370 students, in kindergarten through fifth grade. Our ethnic and socioeconomic population reflects the district averages; we have about 22% free and reduced rate, and our ethnic minority population is 14%, reflecting the district population.

One major difference from school tradition is the calendar. Our students begin school at the end of August, and end classes in late July. We offer an extended year through one- or two-week intersessions approximately every two months, which are optional for students to attend and for teachers to work. (See a sample calendar, next page.)

Huntington Woods Calendar 1996-1997

August 26...................................Teachers report to building
August 27..............Students in grades 1-5. School in AM only
August 28...Kindergarten begins
Aug 30-Sept 2...Labor Day recess
October 17-18...School closed
                      Quality School Conference in Minneapolis
November 6-7...School in AM only, Parent conferences in PM
November 8..................End of first marking period (51 days)
November 12................................Report cards sent home
November 18-27...............................Intersession (8 days)
November 28-29................................Thanksgiving recess
Dec 23-Jan 3..Winter recess
February 6.........School in AM only, teacher record day in PM
February 7..............End of second marking period (45 days)
February 11...................................Report cards sent home
Feb 17-27......................................Intersession (9 days)
Feb 28-March 3.....................................Mid-winter break
April 4-11...Spring recess
May 2........................End of third marking period (43 days)
May 6...Report cards sent home
May 7-8..........School in AM only, Parent conferences in PM
May 12-16.......................................Intersession (5 days)
May 23-30.......................................Memorial Day recess
June 16-20.......................................Intersession (5 days)
July 4...Independence Day
July 17............School in AM only, Teacher record day in PM
July 17, also...............End of fourth marking period (43 days)
                                                  Report cards sent home
July 18..............School in AM only, Teacher record day in PM

This schedule helps students retain more of their learning from spring to fall, so less relearning is needed at the beginning of the school year. Also, without the long summer break, continuity of learning family groups is strengthened, and less time is needed in the fall for students and teachers to get to know one another. Parents and students tell us that the five-week summer break is long enough, because the children become bored over a longer time. Teachers have come to prefer the extended year, also. More frequent breaks are spread throughout the year, with most of our staff taking vacation time during the Intersessions. The result is reduced teacher stress and burnout.

If students attend all the optional intersessions, they receive 210 days of instruction, well beyond the 180 mandated by the state. Response of students and their families is very positive. 90% of students attend many intersessions; fewer, about 55%, attend the summer ones, when many families take vacations. We want it to be a family decision for students to attend but, because we do not have special education, we refer some students to the intersessions for extra outcome-specific tutoring. Teachers have the intersessions, if they choose not to teach then, to rest or to use for additional planning time if they wish.

Intersessions are planned around thematic study, and each is different. We ask students for their ideas of topics they would like to learn about, and incorporate those into intersessions. So far, some of our intersession programs, among many others, have been:

- Spain and Mexico, learning about their customs, history, cuisine, geology, geography, art and music;
- horticulture, with science of plants, planting and cultivation of vegetable and flower gardens, and trips to see farms;
- Black American studies, which included language, African heritage, history, and current issues;
- the continent of Australia, its geography, people, music, animals, and crafts;
- construction, when students constructed a twelve by sixteen foot wooden storage barn for the school.

Having a lot of variety is key to keeping intersessions interesting, and keeping students excited about attending.

We know that people learn best in a supportive environment that helps them meet their basic needs for belonging, power, freedom, and fun. The sections that follow describe some of the things we do to create such an environment, which fulfills the first condition for quality.

Parent and teaching paraprofessional Kathy Van Essen summed up the results of a system designed to help people meet their needs when she said,

> The bottom line is that because teachers, students and parents at Huntington Woods are given freedom, fun, love and power, they feel good about themselves. They want to do quality work, they respect others, they learn responsibility, and are always willing to do better with everything they do. Each person feels like an important part of a big family!

Meeting the Need for Belonging

- **Starting the School Day**

Elementary and secondary schools with which most people are familiar begin the school day by keeping their students outside until the bell rings. This is done so that teachers can have planning time and administrative staff has time for office work before students arrive. But what message do children get when the school door is locked in the morning, and hallways are monitored to prevent any children sneaking into the building early? What kind of environment is established for students when they have to stay outside of "their" school, whether they want to or not, for the convenience of the adults who work there?

At Huntington Woods, we cultivate the attitude that we are here to serve students and their parents. With that guideline in place, our decisions are very often a matter of honesty and common sense on our part. If we say we want this school to serve the students, that means we want to create an environment in which they can feel the

40

strong sense of belonging which is conducive to quality learning. In that case, how best should they come into school each day? We decided that they should be welcomed personally as soon as they arrive, by an adult who is happy to see them.

We enlist the cooperation of parents in bringing their children to school as close as possible to 9:00 o'clock each morning. As a visible sign to our parents that we are here to serve, staff members all park farthest from the front door, leaving the front parking lot open for parents, visitors, and volunteers. We want them to know that this school is here for their convenience, not ours.

When school buses and parents' cars arrive, they stop outside the main entrance, and students walk in through the front door. There is no morning bell. Just inside the building, or out on the sidewalk in pleasant weather, the principal greets each child by name, with a smile. Some of the young people stop to talk for a minute or two, or to give and receive a hug. They then go on to their classrooms, where their teachers meet them with friendly greetings of their own. Parents who walk in with their children are also greeted personally by the principal. Several accompany their son or daughter down the hall to the classrooms; others stop at the office to speak with the school secretary. The atmosphere is friendly and casual; people smile, and there is a lot of laughter and cheerful noise from all the conversation.

By beginning the morning in this way, we start to establish a warm, friendly atmosphere for students, parents, and school personnel. We want each child to perceive that he or she is among friends, and to feel part of a community working together. This helps prevent an adversarial situation developing in which teacher and student find themselves pitted against each other. It also sets a tone of respect for each individual, allowing the children to meet some of their need for recognition and power. This way of coming into school also helps students learn a useful skill for a successful life, because young children often do not know how to exchange greetings. If somebody says, "Good morning," the correct thing to do is to establish eye contact, smile, and give a greeting in return. The two people can then pursue the conversation if they wish to; if not, they go on their way.

Veronica Darwin is the mother of a second-grade student at Huntington Woods, and is also a certified elementary teacher who now volunteers time to work with students. When talking about the morning routine, and also about her impressions of relationships between teachers and students, she said:

> The first day of school here, when my son was in kindergarten, I brought him to school, and I was just amazed. Kaye was outside to meet us. As every child came in the door, she'd give them a hug. She welcomed each one of them individually to school. I've never seen that, a principal being out there and saying 'hi.' Except for the new ones, she knew all the children's names, and asked about their brothers and sisters--she knew them. I don't know how you can know that many kids! She and Jonathan had already met, when I brought him for enrollment, and she remembered both of us. She is so friendly to everyone! And it's not only Kaye, but all the teachers and the staff, too. The adults here really treat the children as people, and not just as students. They are kind to them, as they would be to a good friend.

- **Lunchtime**

Another unique feature at Huntington Woods is our way of "doing lunch." Like the morning entry to school, the lunchtime routine is designed to give students a strong sense of belonging to a caring community, and to teach some useful skills along the way.

Because the "dream team" decided to establish a school day which is not totally clock-driven, lunch period is flexible; learning families can get their meals between 11:45 and 12:15, whenever it is appropriate to their schedule that day. Each learning family goes as a group into the hallway, where the food service worker and student workers have set up serving tables. The young people get their meals on trays, then take them back into the classroom. Their teachers and any parent volunteers or visitors join the children at their tables, where all eat together in a casual, restaurant-style atmosphere. When they are finished, people clear away their lunch trays, and the students clean the tabletops. Because of the student help, only one adult server is needed, and, with no need for cafeteria supervision or cleanup, the cost of this method is low.

Teachers say that in their experience at other schools, lunchtime in the cafeteria is a time when discipline problems frequently occur. In classroom after classroom at Huntington Woods, we see teachers, students, and often a parent or two eating and talking together, and it is apparent that this succeeds as a friendly, pleasant way to share the noon meal. Students are cooperative, relaxed, and involved in conversation. Andrea van der Laan, an upper elementary teacher, mentioned several goals met by having this structure for the lunch period:

> When teachers eat with children, we have that time every day to become friends with students. We talk and get to know each other better, and enjoy some joking and laughter together. If there are any learning family issues that need to be addressed, we can discuss them over lunch in a relaxed, cordial atmosphere. Students come to view us as 'regular people' rather than as bosses, and the sense of belonging and affection is strengthened for them and for us adults.
>
> Students also learn some useful skills and see them modeled by adults whom they like and respect. We get them to practice good table manners (chewing with their mouths closed, using cutlery, and so on), conversation (taking turns speaking, good listening), and being responsible for cleaning up after themselves.

Because only one or two food service workers are needed, and no cafeteria supervisor, this is an affordable way to serve the noon meal, and it helps students and teachers strengthen their friendship.

These are just two examples of design features we have put in place to help everyone at Huntington feel a sense of acceptance and belonging. The learning families discussed in Chapter 4 also strengthen the warm, supportive community in many important ways, staying together from year to year and forming close relationships. The atmosphere is Huntington Woods is noticeably friendly and caring, and this is frequently remarked on by students and parents, staff members, and visitors. Two students' comments are:

- I have a lot of friends. I feel that the environment at Huntington Woods is really warm and caring, and that the teachers care for you.

- A fifth-grade boy, new to HW, was asked by a visitor, 'Are you happier here than at your old school?' The student replied, 'Yes, because people here are more involved, more caring.'

Meeting the Need for Power and Worth

One of the reasons I love this school is that I can come to school and know I will be treated with respect all day, by everyone.
                                        ---Dave, a fifth-grade student

People can meet their basic need for power through succeeding and being recognized for successes. Gaining skills and knowledge is one means of developing power, because it helps students develop a sense of competence and self-worth. Being listened to also fulfills this need; it is important that teachers listen to students and students listen to each other. Working cooperatively promotes listening, and "family meetings" held by each learning family give all students frequent opportunities to have their ideas heard.

Another way the need for power is met is through student-run businesses, which the children manage. Also, the integrated learning system available on our computers allow every child the power and freedom to learn at his or her own level, at his or her own pace.

- ## Publishing Center

The publishing center is an in-school facility at Huntington Woods that carries out publication projects as part of students' course work. Students spend a lot of time writing in class and, through the center, they are afforded opportunities to take selected writing projects through the whole publication process from ideas to finished books.

One student who was working at a word processor in the computer lab spoke about her piece in progress, a story that she had written and decided to develop into her very best quality work, then publish as a book. "I spent a long time improving it," she said, "maybe seven or eight hours since I started, counting the time I worked on it at home." Now she was typing the final version into the computer. Her book will include a page of information about the author, illustrations and acknowledgments thanking people for their assistance, she said, just as a "regular book" does.

The publishing center is a small room equipped with a laser printer, paper punch, spiral-binding machine, and workspace; it is a well-organized facility that enables students to produce a high-quality product. Posters on the walls present dozens of color photographs of students with beaming smiles, holding books they have published. At a table, an adult sat with a student, looking his story. "I want to make the spelling and grammar *perfect*," the boy explained with emphasis, "so Mr. Harding is helping me." Mr. Harding is not a teacher; he is one of several parents who donate their time each week to work in the publishing center. The volunteers help students edit their work, collaborating with them to correct problems and put each sentence into the best form the youngsters can compose.

Another student, Rebecca, who is a published author with two books already to her credit, stood watching as the laser printer sent out high-quality printed pages. "Here comes my book," she said, "and now I'll make pictures for it." She collected the sheets of paper and took them over to the table, then started to draw on one of the pages. Today and at other sessions, she would illustrate the whole story. Then she would bring her illustrated book back to the publishing center where, with adult help, she could punch the pages, then put them into the binding machine and insert a spiral plastic spine. She would very likely keep her copy of the finished book as part of her portfolio, her permanent collection of projects on which she has done her very best work. A second copy of every book is printed and bound at the same time; it goes into the collection of the school library, where it is read and circulated with the other books.

These students all appeared to be focused, absorbed, and enjoying their work. Through publishing, they learn skills that will be useful throughout their lives. They think creatively in the writing process, use visual creativity to lay out and illustrate the books, and practice writing skills of effective syntax, grammar, spelling, and keyboarding. They gain experience in writing for a purpose, organizing a complex project and carrying out a process that requires planning and long-term commitment to a task. Publishing also gives students opportunities to work with others; they collaborate with adults to edit, proofread, and revise their work, and sometimes a student asks or hires another child to make illustrations for a book. With collaboration comes practice in listening, verbal expression, accepting criticism, and incorporating the ideas of other people. Best of all, they get to share their published work with many different people. It can be used to assess progress and set goals for further learning.

In terms of Choice Theory, the publishing process affords opportunities for students to satisfy some of their need for power. Children are empowered through their sense of accomplishment, through seeing themselves as successful authors and receiving recognition from readers, and through an experience in which they and their projects are important--important enough to deserve care and effort, and to have adults come to work with them. The publishing center also illustrates how the basic needs overlap, so that a particular activity might help satisfy several needs. In the publishing process, students experience the fun of exercising creativity and learning new skills, have the freedom to choose any topic for their books and any writing and visual style, and strengthen their sense of belonging through working together and making their books available for others to share.

Staff members and upper elementary students have developed this checklist (next page) to guide students through the editing process.

- **Student hosts**

    People listened to me when I was in front of the state board of education, and when I was in front of a teachers' meeting, and when I host visitors to the school. I feel great! They are looking to me, a fifth grader, and everyone who was older than me was listening to me.

    --a student host

During the 1995-96 school year, over nine hundred teachers, principals, superintendents and board members from around the country visited our school. Our parents keep a bulletin board display titled, "Where in the country are our visitors from?" and students can see all the locations they come from.

One way we have students take responsibility is to host the visitors. Teams of students meet with each group of visitors, give them a presentation and answer questions, and take them on a tour of the school. Hearing about our school from a student means more to an audience of administrators, teachers, or parents than hearing only from an adult. They sometimes seem awestruck by the students' composure and all the things they like about HW. They ask lots of questions about self-evaluation, about how the classrooms are run, how multi-age learning families function, and all aspects of the school. The students are able to respond very adequately, and the adults listen attentively to what they have to say.

Teachers see many instances of children who thrive when they are given opportunities to fulfill their need for power and recognition while in school. One is Alan, whose learning family teacher, Diane Busch, related:

> One boy was having some behavioral problems, and obviously he was not happy with things--I think he needed some power other than what he was getting. My team partner and I found several ways to help him have more control over his school experience. We made sure he had opportunities to speak in our learning family meetings. We paired him with a younger student whom he tutored in reading, and encouraged him to lead the class in some stretching and movement exercises once a week.
>
> Over time, he has come a long way, and doesn't disrupt the classroom any more. Now he hosts visitors. He'll say, 'Hi, my name is Alan. I'm here to welcome you. Can I answer any questions?' The other day he said to me, after visitors were here, 'I didn't get a chance to get around to very many people. One lady just kept asking me so many questions!' He's so intelligent, so aware. Being able to talk to adults like that gives him an acceptable way to use those gifts he has.

He was very excited about being a host. 'Oh please, can I do this until the end of the year?' he asked us...Here he has this opportunity to assert himself in a positive way. Think of the power! He realizes, 'All these adults are listening to me!'

Meeting the Need for Freedom

Many students in our country view schools as oppressive environments with little or no student freedom. Schools are places where teachers tell them what to do, when to do it, and how to do it.

--- Kaye Mentley

The videotape *Building a Quality School: A Matter of Responsibility* presents this student's statement:

This is my first year at Huntington Woods. At my old school, you didn't have any freedom at all. The teacher would just tell you what to do and you would do that. Here, if the teachers have an idea [for an assignment], but you can come up with another one that you would rather do, and it still covers the same things, the teachers will let you. It's okay with them. *They try to work more with you than against you.* (Emphasis added)

The basic human need for freedom can be a difficult one for students to satisfy in a school setting. Our goal is to give students more choices in their learning, and ultimately more control over their environment. They have choices on how to complete assignments, and they have some say in choosing the things they will learn, as later chapters summarize. Students are taught to solve problems themselves, and encouraged to develop personal responsibility.

- **Choice Time**

A significant amount of freedom for students is built into the schedule each day through *choice time*, which follows lunch from 12:30 until 1:00 o'clock. These thirty minutes are duty-free time for teachers. Instead of a noon recess during which all students go outdoors, choice time provides a selection of eight to ten activities, indoors and out. The choices change daily, and each day children can make a new choice. The choice time coordinator posts the day's schedule, and students simply go to the activity they choose. All are supervised by an adult or, in a few cases, by an older student. The only bell of the day rings at 1:00 o'clock to signal the end of choice time.

Choice time activities take place all over the school, in the gym--volleyball, basketball, or sometimes country line dancing; outdoors--kickball, free play, or gardening; the computer lab--games; in the classrooms--art projects, crafts, bingo, chatting, or singing; and in the library--reading books or watching a videotape. Even the corridors are used for one newer choice time activity, hallway wandering. Kaye Mentley explained how it started:

> Several students seemed to be walking around in the hallway every time they had the chance. They would wander up and down, talking and laughing, and it started to kind of bother us. But then I thought, 'Why am I getting irritated about this? It's a harmless activity, unless it takes these students away from class time. How could we help them get what they want in a better way?' So we started a choice time activity called 'hallway wandering.' When students choose this, they have the opportunity to walk through the school in small groups, look at the banners, newspaper articles and student work that we are always putting up on the corridor walls, and even peek into other classrooms. They play follow-the-leader, walk abreast with funny steps and arm motions, or anything else they like. We ask them to respect that some of us are working while they have free time, but as long as they follow the rules of safety and consideration, they can do whatever they want to.

This program is affordable because all the choice time activities are supervised by teaching paraprofessionals or by parents, who volunteer their time. The volunteers initiate activities in which they have an interest or expertise, or can choose to supervise activities planned by someone else. The volunteer roster and choice time schedule are coordinated by a parent or a teacher.

Take a look at a sample choice time schedule:

Monday	Tuesday	Wednesday	Thursday
Soccer Grades 3,4,5 Room 111	**Kickball** Grades 3,4 Room 111	**Soccer** Grades 3,4,5 Room 111	**Touch football** Grades 3,4,5 Room 112
Computer lab Media Center	**Computer lab** Media Center	**Paperbag puppets** Room 101	**HW musical** Media Center
Family Feud Room 106	**Family Feud** Room 106	**Family Feud** Room 106	**Family Feud** Room 106
Pine cone crafts & Fly fishing Room 103	**Marble art & Spinning tops** Room 103	**Marble art & Fly fishing** Room 103	**Spinning tops & Pine cone crafts** Room 103
Outdoor basketball & 4-square Grades 3,4,5 Room 104	**Outdoor basketball & 4-square** Grades 3,4,5 Room 104	**Touch football & Kickball** Grades 3,4,5 Room 112	**Playground** Grades 1,2 Room 110
Playground Gr.1,2--Room 110 Gr.3,4--Room 107	**Hat making** Grades 1,2 Room 101	**Inside basketball** Grades 3,4,5 Gym	**Outdoor basketball & 4-square** Grades 3,4,5 Room 111
Halloween art Room 101	**Playground** Grades 1,2 Room 110	**Playground** Grades 1,2 Room 110	

In our experience, the playground conflicts that often arise during an all-school lunch recess occur much less frequently with choice time, when we have virtually no discipline problems. We believe that giving children the power to choose what they want to do works much better than forcing them all to go outside for a noon recess.

Students' comments indicate that they like the freedom of choice time:

- Choice time is very different here. For recess at my old school, they locked us out. They locked the door, and wouldn't let us in until the bell rang.

- Choice time is very fun! Last year there was a group of us girls who always went together to a different activity every day, until we found one we really liked. I like basketball a lot, so some weeks I played basketball and only basketball if I wanted to. If kids wanted to do something else, they could go to a different choice. Here [at Huntington Woods], they try to find a variety for all the different students.

- I'm an inside-type person in the winter, so I usually stay in at choice time. At my other school before this one, they made us go outside; you couldn't stay in. If they caught you in the bathroom or something, you would get punished. You had to stay outside for recess.

Meeting the Need for Fun

• Student Clubs

Upper elementary students can participate in any of several clubs, which we have started as a way for students and adults to meet some of their need for fun. Clubs meet twice each week for five weeks, during the afternoon. Each is led and facilitated by an adult who volunteers time; parents, teachers, paraprofessional teaching assistants and other staff members can all lead clubs. The available leaders compile a list of clubs to be offered, choosing activities which they, too, will enjoy, and students sign up for a club of their choice. The school principal leads a roller-blading club; other activities include chess, sewing, art stitchery, drama, walking, golf, tennis, jewelry making, singing, line dancing and calligraphy. Some, such as the candy-making club, also run a business and sell their products.

Kathy Van Essen told about her experience as a club leader:

I led the jewelry-making club this year, and I can tell you that these children had nothing but a wonderful, fun time. They had plenty of choices, deciding which club they wanted to join (we had them list a first and a second choice, in case some of the clubs got too big), what to make and with whom to work. They had fun making the jewelry, and it seemed that a big part of their enjoyment was the good time they had learning new things and being creative, with ideas as well as with their hands. Their ideas are really impressive; for example, one day when we were planning to start a new technique using beads, none of the children were familiar with it, and we wondered how to go about teaching twenty-two kids with only two leaders. We all discussed the problem, children and adults, and the students came up with the idea of training one volunteer from each table, who would then teach the rest of the children at their table. We adopted their suggestion, and it really worked well.

They made decisions as a group, such as at the beginning, when we leaders presented a whole assortment of possibilities for jewelry to make; the students talked over the ideas and generated a list of the ones they all wanted to try. We made beads by drying pieces of potato, then painting and stringing them. I had found an interesting book on jewelry projects from nature, and we did some of those, such as collecting and painting small stones, then decorating them with decals or painted designs. We made friendship pins with safety pins and beads, and those became extremely popular. Students loved making up their own beaded patterns, and giving pins to their friends. It was very rewarding to me to see how enthusiastic and involved the members of our club became. They would always wear the jewelry they had made, and seemed quite proud to show it to their classmates and teachers. Each club session would just seem to fly by, and the students were always sorry to have it end. The last day of club sessions, when I told the students that this was the last meeting, they all said "What?!" in disbelief and regret.

Being a leader was great. I had at least as much fun as the students did! I enjoyed looking through all the books for good craft ideas, and learning so many new things, and especially liked the happy attitudes of the students. They were all so cooperative it was awesome. We had no conflicts or arguments at any of our meetings; everyone worked well and followed directions. One boy in our club is a new student this year, who has had some behavioral problems--rather a troubled young person. He came to his first club meeting and sat right down and started having fun, and he enjoyed himself and behaved just fine during every session. This coming school year, several of the jewelry club members are planning to use what they have learned in the club to start a jewelry business for their learning family.

One jewelry maker, Melanie, said,

"It was really cool being in a club. I'm glad I am old enough, now that I'm in the third grade. I love painting the potato beads and making neat jewelry. I wish we had clubs all year!"

- **Discovery Day**

Because bringing fun into learning situations is one of the best ways to engage students in learning, teachers at Huntington Woods constantly look for ways to do this. Ronda Pifer described one idea she and her co-teachers have adopted:

When we design units, many times we'll say, 'Okay, we have to achieve a particular set of learning outcomes. How could we do it?' Earlier this year was one time when, under the pressure of all the specific requirements of the prescribed curriculum, we found ourselves getting away from some of the fun approaches we had been using in our learning family.

So, to get back to that quickly, we asked the students to give us ideas. We had the children list some things that they would want to study, and they came up with a list of topics they were interested in learning about.

We then started having Discovery Days on topics from the list, when we just scrap all the lesson plans and study one thing for the whole day. We chose whales one day. Of course we could not learn everything about whales, but we did whale activities all day long. We studied water on another day. We had a Discovery Day on the Bermuda Triangle because some of the kids were interested in that.

The students are really excited when they walk in and find that it's Discovery Day. We teachers surprise them with it--they never know what day it's going to be. It's usually once a week, sometimes every second week if something comes up. But it's always a surprise, something for them to look forward to. I think it helps some of those sleepyheads who don't like to get out of bed. It has sparked their interest a little bit. They don't want to oversleep on the wrong day!

Helping students satisfy their needs in school is an important condition for building an environment of quality for everyone here. By designing our system with people's survival, belonging, power, freedom and fun in mind, we optimize possibilities for all of us to achieve our best potential.

More elements of a student-centered orientation can be seen in our *multi-age learning families*, which are discussed in the next chapter. By integrating the concepts of lead management in a supportive environment, these class groups form the setting in which students achieve high quality learning.

Students are welcomed warmly when they arrive (below).

Each Intersession
features lessons on a
different theme, such as
Horticulture (left) or
Construction (below).

Students and staff members have fun in the
Roller-blading Club (above), and
in musical and dramatic productions (below).

Student hosts conduct tours for visitors,
including the Computer Lab and Publishing Center
(above)
and a presentation about Huntington Woods School
(below).

Chapter 4

MULTI-AGE LEARNING FAMILIES

Learning Family Meetings
Accelerated Learning
Students with Special Needs
Team Teaching

Chapter 4

MULTI-AGE LEARNING FAMILIES

Human diversity and potential function along a common human development continuum. Individual differences should be viewed and respected as complementary, not degrading.

--Al Mamary (1996)

Can you imagine a school social worker meeting with the principal to say excitedly that, for the first time in five years, he is going to *de*-certify a special education student? How do teachers manage instruction for students of varying abilities? How can gifted students reach their potential in general education classrooms?

Dr. Glasser teaches that strong relationships are necessary for a quality environment that can help all students grow into their full potential. One important way to build relationships is to give students and teachers more time together. Our students join learning families that stay together in the same suite of rooms, with the same team of teachers, for three years, so students and teachers get to know each other very well. Each learning family is composed of students of

59

mixed ages, spanning three grade levels. A typical grouping consists of fifty-four students (grades K,1,2 or grades 3,4,5) and a team of two teachers. A teaching assistant and an instructional paraprofessional work one-half day each in the classroom and also tutor students individually. Parent volunteers are frequently present to help, too.

Use of space in each pair of rooms is flexible because there are no desks for students; rather, children sit at trapezoidal tables that can be pushed together to form hexagons or other configurations. They are named with Spanish words for colors, such as *Rojo, Morado, Verde,* and *Amarillo.*

Teachers base their daily instructional and management interactions with students on principles of Choice Theory and lead management. This means that they lead students without coercing them. To do this, teachers make sure students can feel a strong sense of belonging and worth, make choices of their own, and have some fun every day. They set up appropriate conditions for children to do their best work on meaningful projects, and teach them to evaluate their own work and learning. Adult leaders use learning family meetings to build communication among all members of the learning family. They emphasize cooperative learning, and include students with varying abilities and needs in the learning family without labeling or external programming. By becoming strongly need-satisfying individuals to their students, teachers become part of the children's quality worlds.

Research on multi-age education shows very strongly that students learn better when they are in multi-age groups than when in graded groups (Pavan 1992, Anderson & Pavan 1993, Gaustad 1992). There is always developmental and academic diversity in graded class groups; with the multi-aging system we can accommodate those differences better than we do in a graded system.

For example, Kaye said,

> I think of the first-grade classes I taught. In one class I had children who were at a three-year-old level on their letter recognition, who didn't know any letters at all, and in the same first-grade class, I also had children who were reading at sixth-grade level. But because they were all called first-

graders, the grade system and curriculum pretended that they were all the same. With kindergartners, first- and second-graders mixed together in a learning family, I think it helps us recognize that diversity a little bit more and deal with it better than we might if they were grouped by grade level.

Besides differences in academic development, individuals in any group of students also vary in the ways they apprehend the world and themselves. Such diversity brings intellectual and social richness to the environment, and we welcome it in our learning families. As Howard Gardner writes (1993, page 71),

Cultures profit from these differences in intellectual proclivities found within their population...It has been established quite convincingly that individuals have quite different minds from one another...Instead of ignoring them, and pretending that all individuals have (or ought to have) the same kinds of minds, we should instead try to ensure that everyone receive an education that maximizes hie or her own intellectual potential.

Students know what grades they are in, but no matter what their grade level, the broader range of curriculum and activities in the multi-age group puts fewer limits on them. Teachers do not sort or track students; rather, students can remain in the group until their skills show they are ready to move on (as recommended by Cushman [1990]). They are seldom divided by grade; when smaller groups are formed for particular activities, they are almost always multi-age groups. We only have one teacher for some special areas such as art, music, and physical education, so only about half the students of a learning family do these activities at once, but still as mixed-age groups. Kindergartners, first- and second- graders go together to gym or to music or to art, and third- through sixth-graders go together also.

The continuity gained when students spend three years with the same teachers and most of the same classmates means a smoother transition in August at the start of the school year. Most of the students are coming into a physical and social environment they already know. They feel a stronger sense of familiarity and belonging, and teachers do not have to spend time getting acquainted with them. They already know children's social development, their learning styles and individual personalities, and have established communication, so a lot of time is saved and teaching can get off to a quicker, more effective start. Also, when two-thirds of the students are already accustomed to the rules and routines of a learning family, it helps newer students assimilate more quickly, and students take more responsibility for the classroom environment. Parent volunteer Beatrice Darling notices this in the lower elementary learning families:

> Especially at the first of the year when the kindergartners come in, the first graders and second graders are examples of how to behave, how to sit at your table and how to follow directions, and they help the kindergartners out. We have had new students come into a learning family and decide not to behave appropriately, and the other children will look at them and say, 'Hey, that's not the way we behave in this classroom. Please don't do that!' And wow! The teachers don't have to say anything. The kids say it, because they are proud of their classroom.

Belonging, power, freedom, and fun are all nourished in the multi-age learning family through cooperative learning. Lead-managing teachers (see Chapter 5) support this approach because they have discovered that the more they are able to empower students, the harder they work to learn. Cooperative learning, based on teamwork rather than competition between individuals, provides an environment that enhances self-esteem, thinking skills, and self-responsibility (McCabe and Rhoades, 1988). It has been shown (Rhoades and McCabe, 1992) to "decrease anxiety while increasing performance (page 2). Students learn collaborative skills like those needed by adults, and increase their patience and tolerance of others. They improve their ability to listen, take the viewpoints of others, and state their own viewpoints effectively.

Students speak of working together as one of the important things about Huntington Woods. Cindy and Kyla, two former students who have gone on to middle school in the district, come to HW each week "to help out all the teachers" on mornings when their own school day starts later. Cindy said:

> At Huntington Woods, if you were having a problem understanding something, the teacher would just ask the whole entire class, and then if other students had the same problem, they would hear the answer, too. You can get some help to solve problems, and you don't feel bad about it, like you would if you were having trouble and couldn't ask anybody. At this school, you get to work in partners, and it helps out.

Kyla added,

> If you ask about a problem, the teacher here will ask you to ask two or three different students for help first, and then if you still don't get it, to come back to ask them. Or if you do get it, to come and tell them that. That way the teachers don't have to be in twenty different places at a time. Now, at my new school, we are not supposed to talk in class, unless we ask. The teacher just gives you the lesson and the paper and you have to do it yourself instead of together.

Students who sit together at a table work as a learning team much of the time. Teachers also pair younger and older students for activities to help both strengthen their sense of belonging and recognition. Beatrice Darling commented on the positive self-image that she sees students develop through peer tutoring and helping each other learn:

> I see the children grow in responsibility through helping the younger ones learn. That's evident. When the upper-elementary students are with their lower-elementary student partners, they read together, they do projects together, and the older children think of it as a privilege. They really feel good about themselves, that they got to help somebody else out. My youngest is now a second grader; she gets to help the first graders and kindergartners this year, and she loves doing that. It's part of the belonging feeling that I think we

have at Huntington, and also gives children a sense of importance. The children know that we need them to help, and they see themselves as examples for the younger kids.

We find that keeping children with the same teachers also enhances parental involvement and volunteerism. When children stay with the same teachers for three years, parents more readily build friendly, caring relationships with teachers and with their children's classmates and their parents in the stable learning family system.

Family Meetings

Each learning family holds a daily meeting of the whole group. The meetings, which often take place in the morning, help the school day go better for everyone. They foster an open, caring environment in which teachers and students can discuss issues and expectations and resolve any areas of concern. They strengthen the culture of the learning family and feelings of belonging after members are apart overnight, and children who want to be heard have a chance to talk to the group right away. William Glasser (1969, page 123) has written that, through class meetings,

> Each child learns that he is important to every other child, that what he says is heard by everyone, and that his ideas count. When children experience the satisfaction of thinking and listening to others, they are not afraid to have ideas, to enter into a discussion, and to solve their own problems and the problems of their class by using their brains...Children learn that their peers care about them. They learn to solve the problems of their world.

The meetings used most often are *open-ended* discussions guided by questions the teachers formulate. These are used to strengthen group cohesion and belonging, to help students become confident in their individual expression, and to teach Choice Theory and Reality Therapy concepts. In open-ended meetings, the children "are asked to discuss any thought-provoking question related to their lives, questions that may also be related to the curriculum" (1969, page 134). Teacher not looking for factual answers, but want students to think and relate their knowledge to the topic of discussion. Learning families can discuss plans for the day or upcoming events, and often do team-building activities.

Other class meetings are for *problem solving*; these may be teacher-initiated, or students can bring up any personal, social or academic concerns they may have. Here members can receive ideas and advice from teachers and classmates, or ask for their cooperation if changes are needed. As William Glasser emphasizes (page 129), "The discussion itself should always be directed toward solving the problem; the solution should never include punishment or fault finding." The teacher maintains a non-judgmental stance, but the class makes judgments and from them works toward positive solutions. Once an atmosphere of thinking, discussing, and problem solving is established, situations that ordinarily would cause serious disturbances in class can be handled effectively within the class.

A third type of learning family meeting is *educational-diagnostic*, used by teachers to determine the state of students' knowledge about a subject.

Teachers Ronda Pifer and Larry DeYoung wrote this column about class meetings for the Parent Enrichment Action Team Newsletter, which is sent to all parents:

> Like many teachers at Huntington Woods, we begin each day with a class meeting. Class meetings provide students with the opportunity to express their opinions on a variety of subjects. They also help teachers and students bond in a family atmosphere. The meeting is a tremendous opportunity to solve problems and discuss topics of interest.
>
> During one of our meetings last week, we began a discussion on problem solving at Huntington Woods. The discussion shifted from the problem solving strategies that we use here to those they had experienced in the past. Students talked about detentions, goal cards, stars, writing lines and other forms of discipline. Many felt punishments and rewards did little to change a student's attitudes and behaviors. *In fact,*

they told us that punishment encouraged fighting because it provided attention [emphasis added].

We re-focused the conversation with the question, "If you are not coerced or punished at Huntington Woods, then why aren't you fighting?" We were surprised and pleased with their answers. They told us that there was no need to fight here. Their needs were being met and they knew they had choices. It is a wonderful feeling to know that the changes that have taken place throughout Huntington Woods have made a positive impact on our students!

Teachers plan transitions from the class meeting to the lessons of the morning to provide variety while helping students stay focused. For example, to end one meeting in which a group was learning about the basic needs, the teachers led this closing exercise: The children broke into cooperative learning teams at their tables and had a short discussion about the belonging need. Each group noted a few ideas on how their learning family as a whole could get a stronger sense of belonging while at school. Then the next morning, the teams would report their suggestions to the whole learning family in the family meeting, and the students and teachers would choose some suggestions to try.

Another type of exercise gives students a chance to move around, talk, and stretch a bit before they sit down again. After discussing basic needs, with students giving examples of things they like to do to satisfy each need, teachers might have the students all stand up, walk around, and take five minutes to talk to another student whose example of a need-fulfilling activity each found interesting. This gives children some time to get to know each other better and see if they might plan to do the activity together. Activities such as these help the students to continue thinking about the topics they are learning and practice skills such as writing and interpersonal discussion, and serve as a transition to the next activity of the day.

Open-ended family meetings are not always completely serious occasions. They can also be times for having some fun together, as a meeting of the *Verde* upper-elementary learning family shows. The group had been discussing personality the previous day, and their morning meeting continued that topic in a whimsical, imaginative vein.

Teacher Larry DeYoung: Can anyone else add to our definition of personality?
Student: It's what you eat.
T: Can anyone add to that?
S: It's your actions. Your actions are your personality.

T: Here's our question for today: What if the food you ate determined your personality? Think about this: what kind of personality would you have if it depended on what you ate?
Students:
If I ate Mexican food, I would be hot and spicy.
I would eat Jell-O, because it tickles on the way down my throat, and I like to make people laugh.
Someone who eats seafood would be a fishy person.
I would eat lots of sugar, and I'd be wild.
When some kids eat chocolate, they get hyperactive.
I would eat Jell-O, and I'd be wiggly.
Jell-O, and I would be going all over the place.
If I ate suckers, I would be skinny and round on top.
I would eat carrots, and be ziggy-zaggy like a rabbit.
If I ate mashed potatoes and gravy, my personality would be all warm.
If I ate suckers, I would always fall for people's jokes.
Spaghetti, and I would be slippery.
I would want to eat all kinds of different foods, because I have a lot of different moods.
S: Mr. D., I want to know about you. What would you eat?
T: I like cakes and pies, so I would be the sweetest person.
Student: I want to eat sugar, because I like to be hyper.

T: I have a question for Mike. If you ate a lot of vegetables, what kind of personality would you have?
Mike: A healthy personality. I would be strong.
T: Okay, now everybody turn to your neighbor, and in your smallest one-inch voice, just whisper for a minute.
(Students whisper. After a minute,)

T: Look this way, please. We would like you to go back to your tables now, and put your tubs away. Then stand next to your chair and face the center, please.

When everyone has done so,

T: Ten, nine, eight, seven,
   Look at the ceiling!
   Look at the floor!
   Put your eyes on Kiel!
   Go, Kiel! Repeat after me. Everywhere we go
      (Kiel echoes phrase)
   People ought to know
      (Echo)
   Who we are
      (Echo)
   Shall we tell them?
      (Echo)
   Everybody!
   We are Huntington Woods
      (All repeat)
   Here in Wyoming, Michigan
   If you can't hear us
   (claps twice) We'll shout a little louder!
   (clap) We'll shout a little louder!
   (clap) We'll shout a little louder!
   (clap) WE'LL SHOUT A LITTLE LOUDER!

In addition to the daily meeting, each class also holds unscheduled learning family meetings any time the need for problem solving arises. Students know they can ask for a family meeting at any time if they urgently want to discuss something. As one teacher stated,

> Once we have established a warm and caring environment in the classroom, we can choose any time to hold a class meeting. If a problem comes up for a student and he or she wants to discuss it with the whole group, we can just stop everything, sit down as a group for a class meeting, and discuss it.

Accelerated Learning

Within the multi-age structure, students' interests and abilities determine how fast and how far each one can progress, rather than the limits of graded textbooks or curriculum. We do not do any testing or labeling of children as gifted, just as we do not test or label children as impaired. Rather than referring them to external programs, we serve very capable students within the learning family. Teachers who really know their students can make sure every student is presented with learning activities which that individual finds interesting, relevant, and challenging.

We do a lot of content-area acceleration. In subject areas with very sequential learning, students can use our computer system to progress as far as they want to. The Integrated Learning System is set up so that the children accelerate themselves through different levels in math and reading. We give them whatever they are capable of doing. When they finish one level, teachers put in more software so that students continually challenge themselves. Many of our students are doing sixth-, seventh- and eighth-grade math.

Teachers encourage students to stretch their abilities. Sandy Hartman, who teaches upper-elementary students, said:

> If we see a child reading books that are much too easy for him or her, when we conference, we'll talk about it and help the child evaluate. 'Is this going to help you be a better reader? You read well now. What could you do to help yourself become even better at it?'

Many of our students learn rapidly, and have a strong appetite for information in areas of their interest. When students are gifted with a sense of curiosity about something, we give them the time and opportunity to find out what they want to know. Our students do a lot of informational reading and reports, so we ensure that they get time for researching topics. We have a skilled media specialist who spends time working with the students, teaching them to use the library to search out information. The daily schedule in the classroom can be very flexible. It is not unusual for a child to pick a topic, maybe an animal, or anything that we are studying, and ask, "May I go to the library and find out more?" "Sure," we tell him or her. "Go ahead and find out what you want to learn about."

Teachers encourage active thinking and investigating, and offer their students tasks ranging from simple to more complex ones, including some that are a little beyond their present capabilities. Assignments given to the entire learning family are often structured with two or three options with increasing degrees of difficulty. Students sometimes choose the options they want to do, or at times are assigned the options based on their current level of development or their grade level. For example, excerpted below is a portion of one assessment assigned in an upper-elementary learning family, in the form of a contract with the student and parents, for demonstrating an understanding of maps:

Contract and Checklist for Mapping Assessment

Your job is to create and construct a map of an imaginary place. Today you selected what place your map will be about. Below is a contract that you must fill out and share with your parents. Please have your parents sign the contract and return by
_____.
I have chosen to create and construct a map about
_____
I have chosen Option _____ because
_____

Student signature _____

Parent signature _____

Option 1

Student Teacher
_____ _____   Title
_____ _____   Neat and organized

```
_____  _____   Best handwriting
_____  _____   Compass rose with Cardinal and Intermediate
                     directions
_____  _____   Map scale
_____  _____   Map key with at least 5 symbols
_____  _____   At least 5 labeled locations on map
_____  _____   Attached questions and answers
_____  _____   At least 3 location questions and answers
                     requiring use of directions
_____  _____   At least 2 distance questions and answers
                     requiring use of map scale

              Option 2  (All of the above, plus below)

_____  _____   Labeled coordinate system
_____  _____   At least 3 coordinate questions and answers
```

Besides content acceleration, we also do some grade-level acceleration when appropriate. One upper-elementary learning family presently has two second-graders in it, one who was a first-grader when she joined.

Academically able students have opportunities to act as leaders and mentors in their collaborative learning groups, to tutor classmates informally during the day and with their younger reading partners, and also to teach lessons to the whole learning family. Advanced learners and those who take longer all benefit by taking a teaching role sometimes. They become empowered, perceiving themselves as capable and helpful when they teach and tutor (Katz, 1990). Through helping another student learn, they also deepen their own understanding of the curriculum material.

Huntington Woods teachers are enthusiastic about giving their students opportunities for accelerated learning. Diane Busch said:

> I have worked with kindergartners before, but I never had kindergarten students reading the way they are reading here.

The material is there, and because they see what other students are doing, they ask to do it too. We have three kindergarten students who are independent readers. Would they get that opportunity in another school situation? I don't think so! These young students are doing first-grade work, and they are so excited to be doing it! To be able to offer them that opportunity is just fantastic. I had one little girl tell me, 'I would really like to do Home Link.' This is a math opportunity that the first graders have. 'Sure!' I told her, 'why not?'

Another lower elementary teacher, Jodi Brennan, mentioned other examples:

We have several second graders who are doing math work at a third-grade level. We saw that they had mastered all the second-grade skills, and it is great just having the opportunity to say, 'Well, we have some students who are definitely ready for third-grade math.' And right away, they can do it. They don't have to sit back and wait for somebody to say, 'Since you're doing really well, let's take you out of your regular class and put you into an advanced math group.' We can provide materials for them right here in their own learning family. Also, there is a lot of cooperation among teachers, and our students can go into an upper-elementary learning family for math lessons and practice.

During computer time, they are able to work on ILS [Integrated Learning System] at their own pace. One of our second-grade children is doing at least fifth-grade work. We have some kindergarten children already doing math concepts like fractions. It's amazing what these students can do when they get the chance!

Parents have observed that their children's abilities and individual rates of development are well accommodated in the mixed-age classes. For some parents of high-achieving children, this is a major reason they have enrolled them at this school.

Some parents' comments are:

- Multi-age classrooms were another important factor in our choosing Huntington Woods. There are no limits on how much a student can achieve. I feel assured my children can accelerate to their full potential and will be accommodated by their instructors.

- I am very excited! My children...have an opportunity to learn at the pace of which they are capable without regard to their age or grade number.

- The multi-aging has been particularly helpful for us because my son is extremely advanced for his age. Being encouraged to move rapidly along at his own pace, rather than forced to move along with the crowd, has helped him to greater achievements than would have been possible in a traditional school setting...At Huntington Woods, each child is challenged to reach his or her personal best in every area.

- I feel like our son is in a program for gifted and talented children. He is getting all day, every day the kinds of things his older brother got three times a week, when he was pulled out of his regular classroom for a Gifted/Talented program in another district.

Students with Special Needs

Multi-age combinations work as well for students with impairments as for those who learn quickly (sometimes these are one and the same child). William Glasser, who has worked for many years with children facing major challenges in their families, abilities, behavior and social adjustment, believes (1990) that a need-fulfilling school environment can provide such young people with much of what they need to make extensive changes. The better experiences a child has in school, he asserts, and the better his or her needs are satisfied there, the more strength a child will have to cope with parts of life that are more difficult and less need-satisfying. If children who seem to have the odds stacked against them meet a caring teacher who can help them fulfill their needs in school, much can be done to help them.

This is borne out by the story of one young boy, Drew, who made dramatic changes in his behavior and quality of learning at Huntington Woods. In Drew's case, a move from his original learning family to a new one was the key to helping him improve, along with a planned, cooperative effort by students, teachers and principal to help Drew learn to meet his needs through acceptable behavior.

Drew is a bright little boy who came to us in January. He had some very bizarre behavior--blowing mucus out on the table and showing everybody, belching out loud during lessons, crawling around under the tables making animal sounds--these are some of the milder examples. He was letting himself be goaded into some of these actions by other children. We decided to transfer him to another learning family in the hope that he could make a new beginning. His new teachers and I talked with the students in the learning family about this boy and how they could deal with him. We asked them to think about which of his needs Drew was trying to meet by doing these things; they said they thought he was looking for attention and recognition (the need for power). So we asked, 'What do you want to do as members of this learning family? How can you pull yourselves around him and help him?' They decided that if he did something really bizarre, they would stay as calm as they could, and just say, 'Drew, please knock it off,' not making a big deal out of it, because that would have met his needs inappropriately, but just keeping the tone of things level. Then at the times he was acting appropriately, they would make sure they were engaging him in friendship behaviors, talking to him and giving him attention.

I wondered how frank we should be with these children about the things Drew was doing. But they had heard about his behavior, or would see it themselves soon enough, so we were totally honest with them. And it is working! The children are wonderful with him, and he is doing extremely well considering where he started.

The teachers in Drew's new learning family added:

Before Drew came, we sat down for a class meeting with our students and talked to them about this boy. Basically, we said to them that when they had come in, new to the school, we had taken them as they were, regardless of what had happened in the past. Now we all needed to do the same thing for Drew. 'This is a brand new start for him,' we told them. 'You know how you want this classroom to be, and what you need to do. We want you to welcome him into our learning family and make him as comfortable as possible. He will probably do some strange things that you are not used to, and you need to let him know what is or is not acceptable behavior. Let him know how we want this room to be, and whatever he does, we need to help him out.'

When he came in, he did do some very, very strange things, and the kids were amazingly patient with him. They ignored a lot of it, tolerated a lot of it. Two of our fifth-grade girls in particular have more or less adopted him. We didn't ask them to--they just thought of it by themselves. They said that they would have him sit between them and keep an eye on him, and they did. Every time he did something that was not acceptable, they would tell him, without making a big deal of it, that "that's not something that we do." He was taught constantly the way to behave. He wanted to be accepted, but didn't know how. Once kids were accepting him without the strange behavior, his needs for power and belonging were met pretty well.

There was a day when he first came into our learning family that he lay down on the floor during lunch and he put a slice of pizza on his face. He was yelling, "I'm a pizza! I'm a pizza!" All the kids who were sitting at the table with him were totally ignoring him, while he lay there yelling, "I'm a pizza!" Then when it was time to take the trays out, one of the little third-grade boys looked over at him and said, "Well, we have to take our trays now. And even the pizzas have to go, too!" And it was really something to see. Drew simply got up off the floor, and calmly went and dumped his tray. I think the leadership of some of those children has really been outstanding. The experiences with Drew have brought out some good qualities in all of the children.

Recently the two older girls re-did the classroom-seating chart, which our students change every couple of weeks. They came up to me and they said, 'Is it all right if we keep sitting by Drew? I think we're helping him a lot.' There have been so many times when Drew is just about to go off, and I'm torn between finishing what I'm doing and the urge to race over there, but those children are right there, and they just redirect him. It's unbelievable...*he gets far more attention in a class with fifty-one kids than he would in a special program room with eight other kids* [emphasis added].

Drew has made a tremendous change in a very short time, and I think a lot of it is due to the way the kids treated him from the start. He still has strange behaviors, but he's getting so much better. Even now, if he forgets and does something--it might happen once a month now--the kids will talk to him and remind him. Since he started paying much better attention in class, his schoolwork has also shown a big improvement. He has advanced a grade level in reading, and is making good progress in math and other work.

We just had a meeting of students who want to be school hosts for next year and Drew came to the meeting. He said, "I know you're surprised that I'm here because I'm not exactly a great student, but I'm getting a lot better and I will be better." For him to be able to tell visitors to our school about the changes he has gone through will be so powerful for them, and such a major step for Drew!

Stories like this one lead us to think we are on the right track. It may not mean we will have blazing successes with every single student who crosses our threshold, but we hope to help many, and we will certainly try.

Drew made great progress when his teachers and especially the students proved that they would include him as a member of the family, without encouraging his strange actions. Meaningful involvement with more responsible children who accept him, but not his poor behavior, helped Drew to give up those irresponsible behavioral choices and begin meeting his needs more effectively. Plenty of need-satisfying choices are available to him in the learning family environment. He has experiences each day that help convince him to place many new pictures of successful learning, cooperative activities, friends, and fun into his quality world.

Traditionally, children like Drew would be categorized according to the diagnosis of their problems, and would likely be isolated in special classes for part or all of their school careers. Our approach at Huntington Woods is to include all children in the learning families, and to address their needs with the same kind of group and individualized attention that every other student receives. In reality, *all* children have special needs. In that light, we do not refer students for testing and evaluation, nor do we label any children as learning disabled, AD-HD [Attention Deficit-Hyperactivity Disordered], or emotionally impaired. We think that if a person is given a label, ninety-nine times out of a hundred he or she keeps that label throughout his or her educational career, and even throughout life, with the self, peer, parent and teacher expectations that come with it. Labeling children and isolating them in special education classrooms harms their ability to feel the belonging that they need; other children may taunt and tease them because they are put in a situation that makes them appear different and less able.

Dr. Thomas Armstrong, who has spoken and written insightfully on helping children with attention and behavior problems, believes that

> it is the unique interaction of children's biology with their environment that results in effective and successful learning. We must explore how children learn differently and how we, as educators, can alter our learning environments so as to maximize their full potential as learners... the inability to pay attention or to behave is not within the child. It's in the interaction between the child and the environment....
> (*The Myth of the ADD Child*, Video, 1996)

At many schools when a student has a tendency to be restless, having a difficult time sitting or paying attention, teachers try harder and harder to get the student to sit still and listen for long periods of time. We find it much more effective to give all our students freedom, choices, varied activities, and opportunities for working in

77

cooperative groups so that they get enough time to talk. And instead of always trying to make sure the students sit still, we prefer to build in frequent movement opportunities throughout the day.

We believe that, although there are many talented, dedicated teachers working in special education, the system of referral, testing, classifying and planning is itself flawed, especially when a student must be so far in trouble before qualifying to get help. Why must a child be reading at two to three years below grade level, or have a long list of problem behaviors, before he or she gets some extra help? Accordingly, we do not use external programs for students; our regular learning family teachers work with all students, and with our system of team teaching, the teachers can create opportunities to give students individual attention. Our instructional paraprofessionals are available at all times to tutor any students who need it, without any labeling, without our having to fill out paperwork or try other options first. We can say, "she needs some more practice in subtraction and borrowing," not tomorrow, or six months from now if she is still having trouble, or after we have a psychologist do days of testing at high cost, but right now. It is a very flexible, informal way of providing appropriate support that is highly effective.

The parapros' main mission is to convince the student to see a particular skill as useful and as something he or she wants to learn, to encourage the student to put the skill into his or her quality world. To give a student extra help, they choose methods other than the way the material was taught in the classroom. If an instructional method did not work for a particular child, we find another that *does* work for him or her. It makes no sense to say, "Let's look at that page you were working on in class, and try to do it again." Rather, we say, "Let's sing this song about the addition facts," or "Let's play this phonics game," or "Let's build a model. I will help you read the directions, and you can keep a journal of how you are putting it together."

One of our parapros, Cheri Perez, has started working with a small group of children who are not really 'hooked' yet on writing or reading. To help them have some fun with learning, their main tutoring activity is a business they have formed, called the Creation

Station. The paraprofessional brought in several craft books, which the kids looked through to decide what they wanted to make. Then each wrote a short paper, with Cheri's help, on why they chose to make that item. They decided what their products would be, and how the business would be organized, and then each wrote an application for the job he or she wanted in the company. Now they are going to be making a product and selling it, and we are incorporating the reading and writing.

Children who learn more slowly come to thrive in our learning families, with their warm, supportive atmosphere and readily available tutoring. One brief example of the many students who make terrific progress in this environment is Camilla, a girl who came to us with a label of learning disabled, and had been placed in a special education room half days. Starting at Huntington in the middle of her fourth-grade year, she spent the rest of that year and her fifth-grade year in our school. In that year and a half, she gained 3.1 years in her level of reading comprehension and 2.7 years in applied problem solving. She remained the same in spelling. Camilla is now at the middle school, with no special education services. When we got back a copy of her sixth-grade report card, she had received all A's and B's.

Our teachers employ many strategies that are very effective for students who find it difficult to sustain attention or sit still for long periods. Learning together in varied teams gives students plenty of time to interact, as do the frequent cross-age and peer tutoring. Students become interested in learning reading when each is given opportunities to compose text that has meaning for him or her. Children typically categorized as hyperactive or AD-HD, Thomas Armstrong has said, are often less developmentally advanced in the linguistic and logical intelligences usually valued in schools. Their bodily-kinesthetic, musical, and visual-spatial intelligences are likely to be more highly developed. He suggests (1996) that

> a lot of these kids are physical learners. They need to learn by moving, by touching things, by building things. Many of these kids are picturing image people. They daydream; they

get visual images about things. They look and draw or doodle or work with machines or Lego's. Many of them are highly interpersonal. They need to interact in a social setting in order to learn most effectively...Kids who get into special education classes are kids who think in different ways--who think through the body, for example, kids who are hands-on learners. They need to build things to learn about them. They need to move in order to learn. They need to touch things.

Many of these strategies are features of our everyday instructional practice. We find that not only do they help the learning of children who have such problem behaviors, but they are also appreciated by all of our students. The students also appreciate being invited to participate in decisions concerning their learning and their time in school. This helps all children increase their sense of having a meaningful impact on the world, and so allows them to satisfy their basic need for power. Thomas Armstrong points out that ADD researchers "have noted that many children labeled ADD do best when they are in environments where they can exert some control over their lives" (1995, page 55).

Armstrong further suggests, "Find out what interests your child" (1995, page 82). We do this in our learning families by asking students at intervals throughout the school year what they want to learn, using family meetings to generate lists of these topics, and inviting students to add new ideas to the lists as they occur. Teachers create units, activities and lessons, including Discovery Days, from these lists. By taking inspiration from students' ideas, teachers extend their collaborative planning to include students as well as adults.

Another suggested strategy, "Discover your child's personal learning style" (page 92) is normally part of instruction. Lessons always include activities designed to stimulate learning through all the different modes of intelligence identified by psychologist Howard Gardner (1987, 1993), who believes that there are at least seven human intelligences. We plan instruction so that no matter what learning style a particular child uses most effectively, the curriculum is accessible to him or her. (See Chapter 7, Quality Learning, for examples.).

Thomas Armstrong's suggestion to "use background music to focus and calm" (page 97) is carried out daily in each learning family, with various types of music. The strategy of "provid[ing] opportunities for physical movement" (page 111) is reflected in the frequent use of stretching, energizers, and other physical activities for breaks and also for instruction. With the classroom-based control of scheduling, teachers can take some or all of their students to the gym or outdoors for play and movement breaks when they decide the time is right. Students may choose to stand while listening to lessons. They might alternate between standing at counter-height work surfaces and sitting at tables to do their work, walk from one work station to another, or sit or lie on the floor to read.

Another suggestion Armstrong offers is that adults should "give instructions in attention-grabbing ways" (page 122). One example of this can be seen each morning when teachers Anne Schatz and Jan Lukow wear hats while making announcements, choosing different hats each time—a tall one decorated with peacock feathers, a huge sombrero, a fedora combined with "Groucho" nose and glasses, and others.

The strategy, "Help your child with organizational skills" (page 182) is addressed in several ways. We use classroom calendars, organize and label storage areas, and have students make subject and project folders. We teach them to organize the tubs in which they store their belongings. Upper elementary students each receive a planner book, with which they learn to schedule homework, ongoing learning family projects, and school or family events, and also correspond with parents. Teachers also help students learn to organize their learning through the use of process writing, scientific inquiry, rubrics and checklists, and morning previews of lessons and activities planned for that day.

Many other suggestions in Armstrong's useful book are also matched by strategies used in our school, with positive results for students' attention, learning, and attitudes.

We find that holistic learning experiences in which students actively participate enhance learning for all children, including those with disabilities. Meaningful activities that illustrate how concepts are related across content areas are perhaps most important in helping every student to understand the things we want them to learn. These give the learning a context that the students recognize as relevant to their lives.

One student's parent wrote,

> [My son's] intelligence level is high but he has hyperactive problems and attention deficit disorder [as diagnosed at his previous school]. Instead of being constantly sent to the Principal's office, in trouble on the playground and not challenged academically, my son has been treated as an individual who has value. He has not become perfect, but the methods used to help him deal with life have channeled his great energy and intellectual curiosity in a manner that is productive.

Team Teaching

> Team teaching is where you have two teachers and two classrooms and the teachers work together to teach the lessons in a unique way where it can grab the students and they'll learn. The teachers try to make it very fun for us so that we like science and math, and so we don't get bored in history class. Like, the kids want to get to the action.
>
> --Melissa, Huntington Woods student

The "action" of the teaching team is central to each learning family. Teams of two or sometimes three teachers work together from year to year, allowing the adults more continuity, flexibility and productivity. The team structure promotes the same type of collaboration and cooperation that work so well for student learning. The completely individual control of decision making that solo teachers exercise is relinquished when colleagues work closely together, but they find that the gains in effectiveness outweigh any loss of power. Working together, teachers can accomplish more. They develop a trusting relationship instead of a competitive one, and are better able to meet their needs than when isolated in self-contained classrooms. This enhancement of trust carries over to interpersonal relationships all over the school. New staff members notice a higher level of support than most have experienced previously:

> With both of us being new to this building this year, we've gotten so much support from the other staff members--it's awesome. Their comments, or suggestions, 'Did you do this yet? If you didn't, then maybe you'd want to try this.' It's been really, really wonderful! In the traditional classroom, you were just there by yourself and, you know, 'good luck!'

Teachers at Huntington Woods are committed to team teaching, and have a lot to say about its effectiveness. Ronda Pifer believes that teaming together helps teachers to meet students' needs:

> I appreciate the huge differences between teaming and teaching as a solo teacher. I used to have to go into other teachers' rooms to get their ideas but now, by design, we share ideas with each other. I think it has taken away a lot of the competition. We are not worried about who will look worse or better; instead, we are all sharing ideas in a cooperative approach. It's helpful to have another person we can bounce ideas around with. Larry [DeYoung], Andrea [van der Laan] and I spend a lot of time throwing ideas back and forth.
> Team teaching enables us to teach to different learning styles and to meet the needs of children with emotional and learning challenges. Emotional outbursts have been reduced. I just don't see the need for kids to be pulled out of the classroom with special consultants any more.

Larry DeYoung said:

> We three teachers talk together a lot to plan things. For some students, this may be the first time they ever see a man and woman sit down to talk together and work together, and it

is a good model for them. They see us work as a team, sharing responsibility and coming up with ideas together, the same way the children do in their table learning groups. They listen as we self-evaluate, and learn from our interactions.

The third member of this teaching team, Andrea van der Laan, went on:

Sometimes students try to play off one adult against another, the way they do at home. We have to remember that they are children, and they will try! When they do, we sit down and talk with them about it, and make sure they understand that it is not an acceptable thing. After trying early in the year to play their teachers against each other, they figure out that it doesn't work, and very seldom try it any more. We tell them, when there is a decision to be made, that we work together to decide. I say, 'I won't give you a decision right now, but I will talk to my team members and get back to you.'

Ronda Pifer continued,

It's great having a partner right in the room with you. There are so many opportunities to work with small groups. There are times when Larry will have forty of the kids and I have twelve, and we can do our reteaching that way. Or Larry might have fifty-one of the students while I take one for a little while. Just that whole concept of having such flexibility...I love it.

Support is available if we are feeling overwhelmed, which can happen sometimes. I can remember very clearly a time during the first year here; I was at my desk, and I think there were thirty people surrounding me and they all wanted something. It was just one of those crazy moments, and when I could not deal with it anymore, I said, 'Mr. D, let's switch!' I left and he stepped in, and it was all done in good fun. It was okay with him, and the children understood.

84

We are finding that the more we focus on the children's needs, the better our needs as adults are met. Teaming provides many ways to improve the quality of instruction for students, and also enhances professional performance and working conditions for teachers. Because members of a team work together toward a common goal and share information, ideas, successes and failures, teams come to have a strong sense of purpose and shared vision. Striving together to achieve goals builds cohesiveness, trust and unselfishness. Teachers benefit when there are more hands and heads available to help in all aspects of classroom life, and support is immediate in problem or emergency situations. Because problems are shared, isolation is alleviated, and stress on each individual is reduced. This design allow teachers to feel more peaceful and free, by eliminating that sensation a solo teacher can have of being trapped in the classroom, thinking, 'How can I get out of here at some point during the day?' Team teachers can even take restroom breaks when they feel the need!

Joys are shared as well as problems, and teachers like having someone to laugh with. Personal and professional growth are enhanced when each has another adult with whom to interact throughout the day; the two can coach each other, share responsibility for all children in the learning family, and acquire advanced skills in communication, leadership and conflict resolution. Less direct administrative support is needed, and more flexible scheduling and grouping of students are possible. With the versatility of teaming, a teacher can say to the other team member, "I worked with that 'difficult' child yesterday. She is yours today." What freedom that gives! And how much healthier for that child than having her teacher think with dread each day, "You're mine again!"

Students benefit in other ways, too, in the team-taught environment. For one thing, classrooms can continue to function effectively even when one team member is absent. Also, the personal experience in collaborating that teachers gain assists them in leading student cooperative learning. When students observe their teachers planning as a team, they see skills modeled of how to reach consensus among conflicting ideas, and how to combine each person's ideas to make a final project stronger. Theme and lesson ideas generated by a team of teachers are more varied and more plentiful than those a person working alone can produce, and each member often finds that his or her creativity is enhanced.

With two teachers, said lower elementary teacher Kelli Gatecliff, the human resource base available to the children is much greater. Two of us combining our individual knowledge and styles gives a wider range of teaching possibilities to our classroom. Even more importantly, the teaching team adds a whole new dimension to the students' experience, that of adult interactions. Students watch us talk together and work together every day. They get lots of opportunity to see how we share responsibilities, and one of our goals is always to make sure we demonstrate consideration and respect toward each other, as well as toward the students. With only one teacher, the children would not learn nearly as much about the ways adults work together, so the team teaching gives a richer educational experience.

Sue Schneider teams with Janice Lackey to teach a lower elementary learning family. She said:

Team teaching is very challenging and very exciting at the same time. I would never want to go back into a self-contained classroom. It is much better when you can share ideas with other people. We spark off each other's ideas, so each of us can grow and learn a lot more. Janice and I have very different teaching styles, and very different *thinking* styles, so I have learned so much from her, and she from me. We get the chance to share strengths and weaknesses, and that really helps. We grow personally and intellectually because we are exposed to different ways and learn to be more flexible in our thinking. I appreciate Janice's knowledge about quality schools...Seeing her apply the principles in the classroom has enriched my understanding. I have learned from her example, and from studying and talking with her.

Teaming is also very challenging. Our being two people with very different ideas is an asset, and by the same token, when one of us sees things one way and the other a different way, sometimes it is very difficult to find a compromise. For example, we prefer different daily schedules, so we have learned to talk to each other in advance about what will need to be done the next day or the next week, and who will be responsible for doing which parts. That lets us each start the day at the time we prefer, without one person feeling overloaded if she is here early when the other is not. So we do a lot of compromising. We look at the ultimate goal, which is to help the students have a very successful day.

Sharing the basic philosophy makes this possible. Agreement on philosophy and also communication, especially being willing to listen, are the most important things for team teaching. We ask each other, 'How do you look at education?' and 'How do you look at children?' or 'What do you want? What do you want your environment and learning family to look like?' For example, we want children to be treated with respect no matter which of us they are with, so we have laid down some basic guidelines about how children can learn best and what is best for them. We all work on the process of communication all the time. We learn how to be specific in how we communicate, and we learn more about how that other person thinks. Experience and familiarity with each other's style and approach help us know what we need to do, whether to ask questions to get more specific information, or confirm instead of assuming.

Teaching together for more than three years, Anne Schatz and Janet Lukow have evolved from working independently to cohesive teamwork. Through their experience they have become very close professionally and personally, and now value highly the trust and understanding they have built. Anne Schatz said:

We are a very strong team now. We have come to know each other so well, and talking about *everything* has strengthened our working relationship to the point where we really understand each other. The tougher the situation, the more we communicate. We have worked a lot on developing our communication, talking constantly about our working methods and sharing our private pictures of the way things should be. We were honest about which pictures we were willing to negotiate and modify, and which are non-negotiable. We've gained a lot of respect for each other's vision and abilities.

Jan Lukow added,

Now we understand each other without even using words much of the time. Watching us signal to each other, one little child asked me, 'Do you know sign language?' I told her that we do—our own personal sign language!

I think we have fewer individual pictures now of what we want, and more shared ones. We have a working method of each doing part of a project, then bringing them together into a whole, which works very well. We laugh together a lot, and have a lot of fun.

Anne said,

This has not always been easy, and we have 'walked though some fire' together! But I would not have missed it for anything, and given the choice, I would never go back to teaching solo. Team teaching is better for us and for the students, too.

Our staff members meet the challenges of team teaching by learning over time to use the skills needed to team effectively. They cultivate the characteristics listed below.

Effective team members:
- Treat others as individuals
- Accept and appreciate differences in others
- Are flexible, especially when faced with stress
- Are active, participating, and productive
- Are willing learners
- Communicate in constructive ways

- Are willing to share work, responsibilities, accolades, and failure
- Bring problem solving skills and collaborative values to the group.

We help each other remember that these behaviors can be learned. Our staff makes full use of resources and aids such as inservice training, peer coaching, team processing, and setting team goals for improvement of interpersonal behaviors. By working to increase the effectiveness of all our members, we know we are improving the conditions for our students' learning.

One upper elementary student, Bethany, plans to become a teacher herself, and wants to work in a team structure. She is hoping to teach at Huntington Woods, she said:

> I hope that after I graduate from college, I can get a job at this school. My ideal goal is to team teach with Mrs. Pifer. She is the *best* teacher I have ever had in my life. She says that maybe we could work together someday, and I think that would be really cool!

Chapter 5

LEAD MANAGEMENT

Role of the Principal
Decision-making
Collaborative Planning and Professional
        Development
Lead Management in the Classroom

Chapter 5

LEAD MANAGEMENT

Quality School work...cannot exist if there is an adversarial relationship between those who teach and those who are asked to learn. Not only need there be a strong, friendly feeling between teacher and students, this same feeling is necessary among the students, teachers and administrators. Above all there must be trust: They all believe that the others have their welfare in mind.

--William Glasser in The Quality School Teacher

Can you picture working with students who actively participate in classroom management and problem solving? Or a school in which students, through learning, gain such a strong sense of belonging, success, freedom, and fun, that major discipline problems disappear?

At Huntington Woods, we have changed the system from the usual approach, which says, "Learn, or I will hurt you" to a new approach, which says, "Learn, and it will add quality to your life." We have successfully moved from a boss-managed system to a *lead-managed* system, which focuses on creating a quality workplace. William Glasser (1990, 1994) has developed a streamlined version of the management principles of W. Edwards Deming (1986), which emphasizes the need to improve the system in order to change people's performance within it.

Lead management, which is consistent with Choice Theory, has great advantages over management through coercion. We do not need to coerce students by threatening to fail them, bribing them with rewards, giving them poor grades, or punishing them for not following our rules. Teachers and students are friends and allies, not adversaries. We have found that we can create a school environment in which everyone feels involved, cooperates in planning and mutual support, and continually works to evaluate and improve what they are doing. Students learn avidly, take responsibility for solving their own problems, and experience the satisfaction of doing their very best.

The system of management most widely used in North American society can be called *boss management*. William Glasser (1994) explains its characteristics:

1. The boss sets the task and the standards for what the workers [or students] are to do, usually without consulting the workers. Bosses do not compromise; the worker has to adjust to the job as the boss defines it or suffer any consequences the boss determines.
2. The boss usually tells, rather than shows, the workers how the work is to be done and rarely asks for their input as to how it might possibly be done better.
3. The boss, or someone the boss designates, inspects the work. Because the boss does not involve the workers in this evaluation, they do only enough to get by; they rarely even think of doing what is required for quality.
4. When workers resist, as they almost always do in a variety of ways...the boss uses coercion (usually punishment) almost exclusively to try to make them do as they are told. In so doing, the boss creates a workplace in which the workers and the managers are adversaries. Bosses think that this adversarial situation is the way it should be.

As teachers know, adversaries do not make good students (or good employees). Fun is genetically linked with learning, but the present system of boss management has taken the fun out of learning, to the detriment of both learners and teachers. In fact, many traditional school practices actually promote the notion that learning should be painful to be worthwhile. Creativity, among the most pleasurable of human behaviors, is tied to freedom, and so is also lacking in a boss-managed system. People's creativity and willingness to invest themselves in what they do are actually destroyed by attempts to control and motivate them from the outside. Whether coercion is done subtly or overtly, a student knows when he or she is being coerced, and this creates a climate of fear and resentment.

As soon as this occurs, the child's main agenda becomes resistance, the personal power struggle between teacher and pupil begins, and education is left behind. It becomes a vicious cycle: The child learns less and resists more; the teacher coerces more and teaches less. For many children this adversarial relationship is in place by elementary school, and their formal education becomes secondary to a never-ending power struggle in which all involved are losers.

(Glasser 1990)

In contrast, the characteristics of management by leading are:

1. Lead-managers engage the workers in an ongoing honest discussion of the work that is needed for success. They not only listen but they also encourage their workers to give them any input that will improve quality.
2. The lead-manager (or someone designated by him or her) shows or models the job so that the person who is to do the job can see exactly what the manager expects. The lead-manager works to increase the workers' sense of control over the work they do.
3. The lead-manager eliminates most inspectors and inspection. He or she teaches the workers to evaluate their own work for quality.
4. The lead-manager continually teaches the workers that the essence of quality is constant improvement. To help them, he or she makes it clear that he believes his main job is as a facilitator, which means he is doing all he can to provide them with the best tools and workplace as well as a friendly, noncoercive, nonadversarial atmosphere in which to work.

Lead managers recognize that their main concern is quality, and that it is not possible to force or bribe those we manage into doing quality work. Students might do some schoolwork to avoid punishment, and staff members may follow orders to a greater or lesser extent, but they will adopt the attitudes and exert the effort needed to achieve high quality only when the work and workplace are need-satisfying. A lead manager relies on cooperation, which he or she builds by working on the system so that it can breed confidence and enthusiasm. The lead manager is a facilitator whose job includes making sure the workers have the setting, systems and tools they need to do quality work. Recognizing that people act from intrinsic motivation, he or she makes an effort to combine what people are looking for with what he or she is asking them to do. If the manager succeeds, it is very likely that the workers or students will decide not only to do the work but also to do it well.

If a teacher can convince students to put him or her into their quality worlds as a need-fulfilling person who has the children's best interests at heart, students will trust and care for the teacher and share the goals he or she puts before them. When students put ideas of learning into their quality worlds because they find they can succeed and meet their basic needs through high quality learning, then they are willing to exert the effort necessary to do their best. As William Glasser writes (1993, page 30):

> If there is an axiom to lead-management, it is "the better we know someone and the more we like about what we know, the harder we will work for that person." [Choice] theory explains that we will work hard for those we care for (belonging), for those we respect and who respect us (power), for those with whom we laugh (fun), for those who allow us to think and act for ourselves (freedom), and for those who help us to make our lives secure (survival).
>
> The more that all five of these needs are satisfied in our relationship with the manager who asks us to do the work, the harder we will work for that manager.

Role of the Principal: Modeling lead-management

It is certainly possible to learn how to be an effective lead-teacher, but few teachers will make the effort to do so unless they themselves experience the benefit of this approach. This means that lead-management and the concepts of quality will not flourish in our classrooms unless they are implemented at the level of the school principal. He or she is the crucial element in educational reform.

--William Glasser, 1990

Mrs. Mentley

Kind, caring, making others happy to be in this kind of school.
She's never ever mean at all, she is always fair, fair, fair,
The only thing that she is full of is care, care, care.
She never sits at her desk, she really likes to roam,
Sometimes she even talks right on her little cordless phone.
She looks in all the classrooms to see how we have done,
Three cheers for Mrs. Mentley because she is a lot of fun!!!!!

--student Matt Van Essen

The lead-managing principal has the primary responsibility to set the tone of the school environment. As he or she interacts with the staff, the principal models management style for teachers in the classroom. The principal is a facilitator whose job is to improve the system to create optimal conditions for the work of the school, whether that work is students learning, adults teaching, or conducting the business of the school. Kaye said,

An atmosphere of professional respect and support is crucial if staff members are to achieve quality work. Schoolteachers have an extremely demanding job, so I look for things we can do that will help make it somewhat less demanding. As a principal, it is important to me to protect our teachers' time. I try, as much as possible, to protect them from what I affectionately refer to as 'grunt work.' Any time we can find volunteers or some extra secretarial help to run copies, do word processing of teacher narratives for report cards, and so on, it is helpful.

The leader's job is also to present options for new solutions, and to get input from staff members who are involved in the work being done. Just as it is the teacher's job to create the conditions for quality in the classroom, it is the principal's to create those conditions with the staff members, evaluating by asking, "Are we (as the adults) having fun? How is our love and belonging need being satisfied? Do we feel important in our jobs, and are people listening to us? Do we have freedom to accomplish the goals that we value in our work?"

The staff meeting is an excellent time for a principal to model the kinds of classroom instruction he or she would like to see teachers using. Cooperative learning is used at staff meetings, as it is in the learning families. A principal who wants students to have more fun in class and to be happier in school can set that tone at the staff meetings. Meetings, like learning, do not always have to be all serious business. Including fun activities in meetings and incorporating the element of surprise encourages teachers to choose those techniques to try with their students, because they then realize that those methods are acceptable to the principal.

Just as teachers focus on relevant, useful learning, as administrators, our time with teachers should be focused on relevant and useful interaction. Teachers especially appreciate not spending time on unnecessary meetings or committees. We have worked hard to accomplish that at our school. One of the huge payoffs is that, because teachers see that their time is valued, they are willing to give much more time, commitment, and energy to the school than they otherwise might.

--Kaye Mentley

Meetings are structured to make the best use of everyone's time. They are not used for announcements, constructing schedules, or other work that can be done by memo or by circulating information, so they are kept productive and reasonably fast-paced. We believe that there are four valid reasons to hold staff meetings:

1. *to build and strengthen relationships* by having activities or discussions together. This correlates with satisfying the Choice Theory need for belonging;
2. *to do corporate learning.* For example, all staff members might read a particular book, then get together to discuss chapters or the concepts in it, so that we learn together. Or each studies one area of a book and becomes a specialist in it, then teaches his or her section to the others. Learning together helps satisfy the needs for fun and for power (achievement and competence);
3. *to have fun together.* This need might be met by playing games, singing, doing energizers or other activities, and making sure humor is a part of the discussion;
4. *to make decisions* together as a group.

The conditions that make an effective classroom for students reveal conditions for effective meetings. If students do not find the classroom an inviting place to be, where what is going on is useful and meaningful to them, students tend to be late, not pay attention, disrupt the learning, and otherwise cause problems. Adults are really no different. If the teachers do not find faculty meetings purposeful and useful to them, they will have many of the same behaviors that they dislike in their students. They may come to the meetings late, do other schoolwork, or engage in side conversations while the meeting is being held.

Conversely, thinking about the reasons adults choose these behaviors in meetings can illuminate ways to structure classrooms so that students will want to pay attention and will enjoy their time there more. We try to have a lot of fun at our staff meetings, and we always get them started promptly so that people will want to be on time. They also want to be on time because they never know for sure what is going to happen in today's staff meeting. We never follow a routine agenda, because people like surprises. They like creativity and flexibility. Doing the unexpected, and always working at positive relationships, help the school become a Quality School.

It was certainly unexpected when, at one staff meeting, a person costumed as a gorilla bounded into the meeting room. Amid teachers' laughter, the "gorilla" passed out bananas and handed a balloon to each person. When teachers were instructed to pop their balloons, each found inside a personal note of appreciation that Kaye had written to him or her.

We like to use energizers when we meet, such as this one from one morning meeting: Kaye starts by saying, "Let's all stand in a loose circle. Now, I would like us to go around the circle, and each person in turn, please state one thing you do well, and take a step forward." To begin, she says, "I have strong organizing skills" and steps forward. The teacher next to her then says, "I make it easy for students to feel comfortable and accepted" and steps forward.

Each person in the circle takes a turn affirming something he or she does well: "I know I am a good listener." "I have creative ideas for designing lessons." "I work well with my partner." "I am good at public speaking." "I sing well." Nods of assent meet many of the assertions, and as each person steps forward, the circle draws closer until everyone stands close to their colleagues. Finally, Kaye concludes the exercise by saying, "We have a real depth of talent and skill in our group, and all these things that have been mentioned only scratch the surface. I want you all to know how much I value each of you, and appreciate your abilities and self-confidence. Now, let's talk about our first agenda item." And the meeting proceeds.

Decision-making

Teachers appreciate having an efficient way of making decisions. We use a decision-making technique we learned from Dr. Bob Ludwig, which works very well to ensure fairness and streamline the process. First we talk about the decision thoroughly: would the item under consideration, if we choose to do it, be need fulfilling for students? We also talk over its effect on teaching and learning, and the advantages and disadvantages. Everyone has a chance to express an opinion and have it carefully considered.

Then we get ready to vote; to do this, each person holds up two closed hands, and then, on a count of three, we vote with our fingers. If a person votes ten, it means he or she feels extremely strongly that we should adopt the item. On the other end of the scale, a vote of zero means he or she is strongly opposed to it. We have established a standard that a vote of 80% of available fingers means the item is a 'go.' We know that if we have 80% of our opinion behind it, we will make it work.

Collaborative Planning and Professional Development

In most schools it is difficult for changes to get started because one of the requisites for change--that teachers have time to meet as a group--is not met. Teachers need time to discuss, develop, and accept new approaches, to see demonstrations, and to receive repeated instruction.

--William Glasser (1969, page 117)

The modern curriculum is so extensive that I do not know how an elementary teacher can do it alone now. Without help, how can they design all the lessons to get those major topics across?

-Wyoming Public Schools Assistant Superintendent Bud Pierce

In a lead management system, teachers are regarded as professionals who know best how to practice their art. One facet of the principal's role is to work on the system so it enables staff members to make the most effective use of their time and resources, and do the collaborative planning and decision-making that are important components to Huntington Woods' system. Collaboration becomes especially important where team teaching is used, as it is throughout this school. Opportunity for collaborative planning is built into the schedule by redesigning the time students are in school. Our students have a longer school day on Monday through Thursday, and a shortened Friday. Teachers meet on Friday afternoon, starting at one o'clock and staying together as long as needed. For planning lesson units, self-evaluating, and developing professionally, these weekly meetings are vital. With the principal acting as facilitator, guide and inspiration, staff members use the time to keep skills up-to-date and continue their training and practice in Choice Theory and reality therapy.

We begin planning as a whole-faculty group, then break into upper- and lower-elementary units, and finally have a period of time to work as learning family teams (teachers and assistant). Diane Busch talked about how the system of collaborative planning works:

> The sharing of lesson plans has been very helpful. When we had a set of eight science learning outcome goals to meet this spring, each of us chose one of the standards and planned a lesson around it. It has been wonderful sharing ideas. I don't think that by yourself you could ever develop as many units. I couldn't create eight units in one year to the depth that they have been done. But since everyone was so willing to share and encourage each other, it has worked out well for each teacher.
>
> And then the care for the children! In so many school situations the attitude of the teachers is, 'This is my room and these are my students, and I'm blind to anything happening with anybody else's children.' Here, the spirit of sharing is magnificent. Everybody is always ready to try to help everybody else's children.

Andrea van der Laan wrote in an article on self-evaluation and lead management:

> To help us the first year [in collaborative planning meetings] Kaye would often have us sit with team members and answer tough questions and work out individual differences. We would talk about the workload, consistency problems, and any other teaming issues that arose. Kaye helped us by constantly focusing us in on what we wanted, what we were doing to get there, and what we said we would stand for. She taught us how to lovingly confront and how to negotiate with one another.

At many staff meetings throughout the year, the principal leads teachers in practicing skills in reality therapy, reflecting on the conditions for quality, engaging in self-evaluation, and discussing ways to improve lesson design. To be effective, staff training cannot be a single, one-time event. Staff members have found that hearing something new at one in-service session or professional development workshop does not really carry over into positive change in the classroom. If something is important enough to take time to learn, we believe it is important to make opportunities to practice and discuss it. Creative planning by the principal helps make these sessions interesting and fun for the participants.

At one collaborative planning meeting, Kaye conducted a role-playing practice exercise, with a twist. She described it like this:

> One Friday I had written descriptions of three different scenarios and put each into a balloon. I had teachers count off by threes so they were in three groups, each with a balloon. Before they popped their group's balloon they got to decide if they wanted to keep it or trade it with another group, if they could find one willing to trade. Then they popped the balloons, and found a scenario to play out. One was of a teacher who was choosing to frustrate over student behavior. Another was a principal who was complaining because sometimes colleagues criticized his school, and the third was a child who did not think his teacher liked him. So they played those parts for the whole group, with one teacher playing the role of counselor. Then the others were asked to give feedback to the actors, on questions such as 'What would you think if you were a teacher overhearing this conversation?' and 'What would you think if you were a parent overhearing this conversation?'
>
> We do those kinds of things to continually strengthen and refocus our understanding of Choice Theory. When you have lived external control psychology all your life, as we all have, it is all you know. You know complaining, you know blaming and criticizing, but you don't know taking control of your own behavior. We remember that you can only control yourself; you can not control anybody else no matter what you do.

- **Reversing roles: principal for a day**

Fifth-grade students get a closer look at the leader's job when they shadow the principal for a day. (The principal also shadows a student for a day to see Huntington Woods from a very different point of view.) The student arrives earlier than usual in the morning and stays with Kaye all day, observing and helping her with all her tasks. Summarizing their experiences, some have written:

- To be a Principal it takes hard work and a good grasp of a kid's view of things or you can never be a nice, caring, fun loving, playing principal. In my studies I have seen nice, mean and wicked principals, but one meets up to my standards...Mrs. Kaye Mentley, my principal.

- Mrs. Mentley wanted me to talk to these two kids that had an argument. I took them in another room and talked to them. They talked and solved their problem, so I took them back to their room. I think being a principal is a lot of work but fun at the same time. A few of the things you need to be a great principal like Mrs. Mentley are: be a hard worker, get to know the kids, and act like a friend, which Mrs. Mentley always does. I think she is a great principal and always works hard.

- I learned that a principal is very busy and does a lot of walking around. She has to answer the phone and call people. She talks to kids who make wrong choices. I would like to be a principal because I would get to be in charge of the whole school. I would like to have my own office with a computer and my own phone. I would not like to be a principal because it would be too much work and I would have to walk around all the time. I would have to get up early every morning to go to school before everyone else. I think Mrs. Mentley makes a good principal because she is kind.

A school superintendent in one conference audience asked the Huntington Woods students during their presentation, "I understand from your talk what the students' job is, and what the teachers' job is, but I am not sure what the principal's job is. What does she do?" The two girls looked at each other, and back at him, and said, "Well, she hangs out. She walks around, comes into the classroom and talks a little bit, then she leaves and goes somewhere else, then pretty soon she comes back--she just kind of hangs out at school." Another student counted the times she saw her principal in the course of one typical school day. From the greeting in the morning at the door through Mrs. Mentley's visits to her classroom, once or twice at choice time, in the hallway, to "good-bye" at the end of the day, her count was fourteen times.

These students have each remarked on one of the central characteristics of effective leadership: to be present where the work of learning is going on, observant of the ways people's jobs are structured and how they do them, available for consultation about questions or problems, and always modeling involvement, caring, and, tactful responsibility.

When I walk around to the classrooms and observe the way things are going, Kaye Mentley said, first I want just to see what is happening. If I see problems or places for improvement, I do not comment or make suggestions right away. First I try to see more completely what the situation is, and think for awhile about the best way to improve it. My job as leader is to present options for new solutions, and also get input from staff members who are involved in the work being done.

To gain the close rapport needed for a friendly and supportive workplace or classroom, one thing a lead manager does is openly talk to those managed about the kind of person he or she is and what he or she stands for. It is best to be explicit about people's roles in the workplace, and make clear what the manager will ask workers to do and will not ask them to do, what she or he will do for them and with them, and will not do. Kaye asks staff members what they want from her as a principal. She also specifies what she will do for them, and what she will not do.

Another part of the principal's role is communication with parents; see the chapter on Parental Involvement for more about this.

Staff members comment about the principal's role at Huntington Woods.

- Teacher Marilyn Spreng:
  A big part of our success is due to our principal, Kaye. We need someone committed, a lead manager like she is. The way she gets our energy going, her rapport with people, the way she treats her staff - all of that really makes it work. She treats staff as friends. She doesn't coerce. She is very clear, and we know what she wants, but she will bend over backwards for us, too, and it's just a give-and-take. We all are here for the children. She talks out problems with us, the children, the parents, and shows us how to practice what we preach.

- School Secretary Sally Fleming:
  Before our days at Huntington Woods, I saw how Kaye could motivate people, even with a staff who were not in agreement to begin with. In spite of the reluctance that some of them might have felt, they were willing to try things her way because she is such a good support. She goes out of her way to help teachers in time management, classroom advice, and any way she can. She finds ways to make their work easier.

- Andrea van der Laan:
  I think the staff at Huntington would agree that we are not finished with the change process yet. Kaye still asks us tough questions about what we are doing, why we are doing it. Is it in the best interest of the children? Can we do better? She continues to model the Choice Theory, reality therapy process to help us solve problems. She continues to help us grow as we work our way towards quality.

- Kathy Van Essen:
  Kaye's strong leadership is never a "dictatorship." Her type of lead management allows everyone to be a leader, not only teachers, but parents and students as well. She is always looking for the positive or the strong points in everyone from staff to students, and makes everyone feel like they are a part

of the family. She is always willing to change or try new ideas, and gives everyone the chance and choice to do the same.

In 1996, our staff compiled suggestions in this *Principal Wish List*, and also gave students an opportunity to contribute their ideas.

Principal Wish List

What do teachers want in a principal?

A vision for the school; think in terms of the future; long-range planner
An objective total picture of what is happening in the building
Give time to work with students
Non-judgmental listener
A dreamer
Passionate and caring with students
Have a sense of humor
Get to know the students, parents, and families
Be everyone's friend
Problem solver with lots of ideas
Sharing ideas for problem 'fix-ups' in a loving way
Understands the many functions of teachers; protects their time and
    energy

What do the students want?

Someone who can handle a lot of different problems
Nice
Have all kinds of activities for kids
Talk to students often
Have fun with kids
Outgoing
Be fair
Smell good
Be there when kids need him or her
Be helpful
Have nice hair
Problem solver

Lead Management in the Classroom

The lead-manager teacher, who understands [Choice] theory and applies the questioning strategies of reality therapy, abandons as counterproductive the inclination to exercise forceful authority over the learners. The lead-manager teacher transfers the responsibility for acceptable behavior to the behavers—not through force or domination but through reason and support.

Crawford et.al. (1993, p 185)

William Glasser (1990) teaches that managing people, even for a skilled and creative manager, depends for its ultimate success on the cooperation of the people being managed. With students, a group whom many teachers perceive as being highly resistant to being managed, the emphasis on self-responsibility for behavior and learning is especially important. Through changing the environment and system to help students meet their needs, and using strategies of reality therapy to help young people create solutions to their problems, staff members at Huntington Woods are developing classrooms which support all students in meeting goals they themselves help to define.

Glasser has observed that for people learning the skills of lead-managing, learning to supervise noncoercively, for example, asking rather than telling, is one of the hardest parts of the process. He writes (1994, page 100):

Fueled by a lifetime of exposure, starting in our homes, accelerating in our schools, and peaking in many of our work experiences, coercion has become so ingrained that is literally a part of what most of us consider to be common sense. Even though it is so destructive to the goal of quality, it seems so right.

Our teachers understand that coercion does not succeed in motivating anyone. Threats of punishment or failure leave students anxious and resentful, and promises of reward decrease their awareness of the real reasons for learning and responsible behavior. (For an illuminating explanation of the negative effects of reward systems as motivators in schools, see Alfie Kohn, *Punished by Rewards* [1993]).

Experience confirms that no amount of preaching, rewards, or punishment can make students want anything. Only students can put pictures of school, teachers and learning into their quality worlds. To influence them to do this, we focus on fulfilling the conditions for quality in the learning family: a supportive, need-satisfying environment free of coercion; meaningful, useful learning; and self-evaluation. Workers, whether teachers, staff, or students, take ownership of their tasks when they have effective input. A lead manager should ask a worker for help when he or she notices any kind of problem and, William Glasser advises (1994, page 38),

> If [the advice] cannot be used as given, you should use as much as you can and thank the worker for what he suggested. If possible, also explain to the worker why only some of the advice was usable, and from this honest discussion the worker can learn more about the broader implications of the job. Keep in mind that when a worker learns that any of his advice was useful, that knowledge will spur him to work harder and quality will increase.

This is in agreement with the advice of Thomas Lickona (1991), who has written about the importance of educating for character in elementary and secondary schools. To help a school create a positive moral culture, one of the elements Dr. Lickona recommends is democratic student involvement that "fosters the feeling 'This is *our* school, and we're responsible for making it the best school it can be.'"(Page 325).

Students have opportunities to have input into their schoolwork in several ways. Evaluating their work, rather than simply being evaluated and given a grade by the teacher, is one crucial element.

Contributing ideas for topics of study is another. Teachers ask students what they want to study, particularly at the beginning of the school year, and use their responses to plan units and lessons.

Even for particular assignments, children have some say in what they are doing. We have a policy of alternative assignments in all learning families. If a student does not find an assignment interesting, or does not want to do it for some other reason, he or she has the right (and the comfortable relationship with the teachers) to go to them and say, "I really don't want to do this assignment." The teachers then say, "Okay. Here is the learning that we are looking for." They describe the learning outcomes they want the project to demonstrate, and ask the student, "How do you want to do it? Would you like to design another way to show that you have learned these things?" If he or she can develop another suitable project, that is very acceptable.

Student input on how to make school more need-satisfying is something we continually look for. As students learn Choice Theory, we discuss the basic needs and ask them for examples of experiences that help them meet those needs in school and at home. From their examples, and from areas in which they mention few examples, we get valuable information on whether the children perceive that their needs are being met in the learning environment. We need to ask the students. We adults may think they have freedom, or are meeting their need for power, but it is *their* perception that matters.

We believe that when problems arise, the people closest to any problem are the ones best able to fix it. We have decided, rather than employing a full-time counselor, to provide the training and time needed for each teacher to talk through problems with students. Learning reality therapy provides the training. To give teachers the time to work with students individually, the school hires a substitute teacher one day each week. During that 'counseling day,' classroom teachers choose a time for the substitute to teach in their place, freeing them to meet with students. A teacher can use this time to talk with a child who is having a problem of any kind, or chat with a child who is shy or reserved to get to know that student better. In such a conversation, a teacher can learn how well the student is meeting her or his needs in school.

Lani Dykhouse had a meeting like this to counsel one of her second-grade students, Ashley, who had sometimes been choosing disruptive behavior during lessons. At the agreed-upon time, the teacher and student took a walk together outside to talk things through in a calm setting. The conversation began on general topics, with Lani speaking in a friendly tone and listening attentively, to establish a cordial mood and encourage Ashley to speak frankly.

Presently, Lani said, "Tell me a little bit about school. Do you have friends here? Who at school really cares about you? And whom do you really like?' Ashley said, "Carrie and Nicholas are my friends. We always play at choice time. And Mrs. Spreng really likes me, because she gives me a hug when I come in." Her reply helped Lani to assess how Ashley is meeting her need for belonging. She asked the child some questions about fun: "What things at school do you really enjoy? What is your favorite time of the day? During your favorite time, what is happening that you enjoy? Is it outdoors or inside?' Then she listened to the answer, checking for fulfillment of the need for fun. "When in the school day do you get to pick what you want to do and how to do it?" she asked next, and listened for the freedom need.

They conversed in a casual way that allowed the teacher to judge whether, in this school and in her classroom, Ashley can satisfy her needs. When the teacher asked, to assess whether Ashley was able to satisfy her need for power, "Are there some times in the school day when you feel really important and you feel like other people are listening to you? When is that?" Ashley could think of only one time that she feels important. She answered, "On the day when Vanessa comes and we read." (Vanessa, a fourth-grade student, is Ashley's reading partner.)

The two had by then come to the playground equipment, and Ashley asked, "Would you please push me on the swing?" Lani Dykhouse, thinking that she had learned some useful information and that this was enough for this young child today, agreed to push Ashley ten times before they went back inside. This gave both of them a chance to share a little fun.

Later, she discussed the session with the other learning family teachers. They agreed that Ashley probably was not getting enough power in her day-to-day school experience, and was distracting other students in an effort to gain importance and attention. They decided on a few things they could do to help her meet that need better. Ashley would be the one to lead the line of students the next day when her group went to the Media Center, and they would ask her to feed Sammy, the learning family's pet guinea pig, all the following week. They planned to make an extra effort to encourage Ashley to speak during family meetings to give her more chances to be heard. They know that when a student like Ashley can satisfy her needs in school, then she can begin to do quality learning. It is each teacher's job to create the conditions for that to occur, and we take that responsibility very seriously.

When a student has problems in a particular subject area, or tends to choose disruptive behavior during those lessons, during their talk the teacher might ask, "What would help (math) go better for you? What things have we done in math that you liked? Which activities have really helped you understand the lesson?" This kind of questioning can spark ideas for helping the student enjoy the work more and become more involved in it.

Staff members and parents share a belief in the importance of helping children grow into responsible young people of strong character. Since we do not think there is any such thing as a value-free or value-neutral education, we work together to define values that we want children to learn, and together develop the standards of conduct for everyone at Huntington Woods. The Parent Handbook includes the following summary of rules and outlines the discipline sequence.

Getting along at Huntington Woods

The staff members at Huntington Woods have devoted a great deal of thought and discussion to how we want to get along at school. We believe that all problems with students or adults can be solved by talking them through and that no one needs to feel hurt. We have decided to use the concepts discussed in Dr. William Glasser's Quality School, Choice Theory and Reality Therapy.

We have developed the following rules for our school.

1. COOPERATION: We believe that by working together, we will have better quality work and learning. Cooperation means listening to each other, sharing ideas, and each doing our part.

2. CONSIDERATION: We believe that when we treat each other kindly, we will have more friends, get along better, and be the kind of people we want to be. Consideration means saying only good things about and to other people, and helping other people out when we can, and treating people with respect.

3. CONSERVATION: We believe that our property and our environment are important, and we will take care of them. Conservation means that we recycle and don't destroy things.

4. SAFETY: We believe that we learn and work best in a school where no one gets hurt. Safety means that we are careful not to hurt others, and we solve our problems by talking them through.

All students have been taught these rules through discussions with their teachers, role plays, and by having learning family meetings with Mrs. Mentley.

We believe it is imperative that we provide an emotionally and physically safe environment for student learning. We have decided that at Huntington Woods there will be no verbal or physical abuse, including comments that students occasionally make in an attempt to be funny.

> If students talk disrespectfully (in tone of voice or by what they say) an adult will give the student the "T-sign." This is the sign used for time out in athletics. That signal means that what the students is saying doesn't sound very good, and he/she needs to try again. We believe that respectful communication is an important skill for success in life.
>
> Students who stop the learning of others will be asked to sit apart from the group. As soon as the student decides his or her behavior will help the learning of others, the student may rejoin the group. If the student still stops the learning of others, he/she will be removed from the class. After a time, if the student decides he/she is ready to let others learn, he/she may go back to class. If the student is still disruptive, the parents will be contacted to remove the child from school until the child is willing to help others learn.

Parents have also identified values of respect, honesty, courtesy, and the understanding that one's actions impact oneself and others as ethical principles they and Huntington Woods School will teach their children. The values and rules are discussed in every learning family and applied consistently on the playground, in the hallways, and on school buses as well as in the classrooms.

They are also followed and modeled by the adults in school in their interactions with each other and with students. (See Lickona [1991], pages 325-347 on the need for consistent school-wide commitment to moral culture.) One important change we have made is to leave behind the separate sets of rules for teachers and for children that schools so often have. The message we want to give our students is that they are worthy of care and respect. They do not have to earn the privilege of respectful treatment by putting in a certain number of years of life. We do not consider them less than fully human just because they are young, so we work hard to have consistent rules. If it is acceptable for the principal or teacher to have a water bottle or a cup of coffee, it is okay for our students to have their water bottles. Adults do not cut into lines ahead of children, interrupt them, or speak sarcastically or disparagingly to them, just as they never would do to a colleague. We believe all problems will be solved by talking them through, so we would not say to a student, for example, "you talked too much during math, so now you owe me some time." Addressing teachers, Kaye Mentley elaborated:

> If a teacher, 'Jane,' came ten minutes late for a staff meeting, can you imagine Jane's principal saying to her, 'now you owe me ten minutes because you were late for our staff meeting'? Too often educators say those things to our children and then wonder, 'why don't children love school? And why does it seem so adversarial and we are working against each other?' Picture what would happen inside you as a teacher if your principal, usually in front of everyone else, were to say, 'I noticed you two talking while I was talking, so now you owe me some time,' or some of those other things that just seem to roll out of our mouths when we talk to children.

On the wall in one room is a large poster which students have made of the "Keys to a Happy Learning Family," which are also the four school rules. A drawing at the side illustrates each one:

Cooperation - Is it helpful?
Consideration - Is it kind?
Conservation - Could it waste or destroy anything?
Safety - Could anyone get hurt?

In keeping with the lead-management principle of openly discussing roles, we find it extremely helpful to establish together what we want for the school year when we begin school in August. Teachers talk over expectations with their students, and students contribute their ideas for behavior and attitudes that will help learning. We hold this type of discussion in a series of learning family meetings, often over three days during the first week of school. (See the newsletter *Quality Connections* [1997] for suggestions on creating a warm, caring environment at the start of the school year, including a description of this process.)

On the first day, teachers lead each class in discussing everyone's vision for a successful year, using questions such as, "If at the end of this year you were to say, 'Wow! That was my greatest year in school ever,' what would have happened during the year? What would you have learned and done, and what would the classroom have been like for you to say that?" The teacher records students' responses on a large sheet of paper, adding his or her own ideas as well. This description of quality world pictures of a terrific year is then posted on the wall.

At the next class meeting, the learning family works together to formulate "job descriptions" listing responsibilities of teachers and students. To guide the discussion, the teacher might say, "If what we really want are the things we listed here on the wall, let's talk about what my job might be to help us get that, and what your job might be." Here, the teacher will need to listen carefully, and use questioning techniques; if this is the first time students experience an activity like this, they will usually say only what they think the teacher wants them to. It is important for them to trust the teacher and to know that he or she truly wants to work this out together. Things that are not the teacher's job are listed, then things that are and are not the students' job. The page is then posted on the wall with the first one. Here is an example from one classroom:

My Job - the Teacher	Your Job - the Student
Teach kids	Be an active listener
Help kids learn	Do quality work
	Follow rules
Teach procedures and rules	Be safe
Help kids when they get hurt	Be considerate
	Be cooperative
Display work	Conserve
Evaluate work	Evaluate my work
Talk to parents	Talk to parents
	Clean up after myself

The third day's activity is to talk together about what procedures (rules) the group can agree to that will help them get the classroom experience that they want. Again, the lead-managing teacher adds ideas along with the students. Often, newer students who have had experience in an external-control environment begin to suggest punishments that they think should be in place if someone does not follow the procedures. The teacher then talks to the class about his or her belief that all problems can be solved by talking them through, and might do a role-play with a student to demonstrate how this would occur. This gives an opportunity to show how the questioning process of reality therapy is used to help a student evaluate whether his or her own behavior is living up to the agreed-upon procedures.

The finished page is then posted with the others. All three should be kept short and simple, in language that everyone can understand. The lists can be referred to as needed to help keep everyone on track toward their goals. They are also used in a positive way, to help students (and teachers) give themselves credit when they *are* doing the things that will help everyone move toward their goals. In keeping with the use of self-evaluation for continuous improvement, teachers stress to the students that these documents can be revisited, changed, and improved throughout the year. At any time, a student or teacher can bring them up for further discussion.

Diane Busch, a lower elementary teacher, said,

> Sometimes when we need reminders of what their job is and what our job is, we just stop what we're doing and say, 'Class meeting!' We all will stop and talk about whatever the situation is and try to talk it through. We ask them questions about supporting learning: 'Are you going to support learning today? What does it mean to do that?' The students know! They come up with wonderful explanations of what it means to support learning and what they need to do to support it. Or we get them to compare their behavior with the four keys to a happy learning family, which are basically the four school rules, and see if they are being cooperative, and considerate, using things or time wisely, and being safe.

When lead-managing teachers do these kinds of things to help build the perception that the learning family belongs to the whole group, we find that students take on responsibility for the class environment. Sandy Hartman, an upper elementary teacher, mentioned this example:

> At the beginning of the year especially, the fifth- and fourth-graders tell the third-graders how things are done. One time, a younger child was doing something unacceptable, and the teacher just gave a hand signal to a fifth grader who was there. The older student nicely told the younger kid, 'We don't do that here. This is our classroom, and we want it the way we like it, so we don't act like that.' So the students start taking ownership... The teacher does not have to handle all the discipline, and that kind of thing is much more powerful coming from their peers than from an adult.

Students work toward quality participation more readily when they know what quality looks like, so teachers model the kinds of behavior we want students to choose, as well as explaining it. For example, students are responsible for paying attention during a discussion; their teachers ask them for very specific behaviors, and demonstrate them at the same time. They might say, "Please check your body language as you are waiting to answer the question, and make sure you are giving your best attention. Eyes looking at the speaker, mouth quiet, ears listening?" Concurrently, they model what they are describing, looking at and listening attentively to each student who contributes to the discussion, often leaning a little forward, and refraining from interrupting. This helps create an atmosphere of respect and cooperation that is need-satisfying for everyone.

Teachers have developed several ways to get students' attention while maintaining a non-coercive tone. One, which we call "Give Me Five," can be seen in action in one learning family: the teacher goes to the center of the two rooms where all students can see her and asks, "Okay, boys and girls, will you get ready to give me five? One, two, three, give me five!" Students put down their pencils and on the count of three, clap their hands once, raise one hand in the air, and look toward the teacher. In this instance, a few still talk to each other; the teacher, looking around, says, "Some of you are paying good attention, some not so good. Let's try it one more time and see if we can do better. Talk for thirty more seconds, and be ready." A buzz of conversation rises until she says again, "One, two, three, give me five!" This time everyone claps in unison, all raise hands, and the room becomes very quiet. The teacher, holding up her hand like everyone else, looks around the room and says, "Did we do better? Ask yourself how you and your table partners did this time."

We think it works best to teach the use of any tool or procedure such as this one *before* it is needed, with students, personnel, and parents alike. Teachers lead students in talking about the need for attention, and practice "Give Me Five" from the beginning of year, so when the need for it arises, everyone is familiar with the behavior we expect of them. Visual aids also help integrate these tools into people's repertoire of behavioral choices. Among the posters on the wall in this same classroom is one made by the students that lists and illustrates the components of "Give Me Five:"

1. Eyes on the speaker
2. Mouth quiet
3. Be still
4. Hands free
5. Listen

Clapping hands in rhythm is another method for gaining the attention of a group. A teacher begins clapping: clap, clap, clap-clap-clap. As he or she repeats this pattern, those who hear it stop what they are doing and join in. As they do, the clapping becomes louder until everyone realizes what is happening and claps along. No one is singled out by name or otherwise embarrassed, but the group is ready to hear what the speaker wants to say.

When students' side conversation interferes with someone being heard, the *Oro* teachers use these non-coercive techniques: during a learning family meeting one day, Michael was contributing to the class discussion, but someone's talking drowned out his statements. Teacher Kent Snoeyink asked him to wait a moment, and said, "Everybody say, 'Michael, will you please repeat your comment?'" The whole group chorused in unison, "Michael, will you please repeat your comment?" Michael, smiling, repeated what he had said. Or, in another instance, co-teacher Sandy Hartman said to the students, "And suddenly a hush falls on the crowd...one, two, three, Hushhh!" with everyone joining in to say "Hushhh!"

When a student behaves in ways that prevent others from learning, a teacher might say to him or her, "Please go and *take a rest*." The students know what this means; the child gets up, goes over to a big wooden rocking chair at one corner of the room, and sits down. He or she sits for a few minutes or longer, then comes back and rejoins the group.

No one tells the student how long to sit there; each knows that his or her job while taking a rest is to think about what he was doing and whether his behavior fit with the rules of consideration, cooperation, conservation and safety. It is also to think about what he had been trying to get by his behavior, and develop a plan for getting what he wants in an appropriate way. The child is responsible for deciding when he or she is ready to come back to the group and choose more effective behaviors that will support learning.

To involve students further in the management of the school, we consult them when selecting new members for our teaching staff. Teacher candidates give a demonstration lesson to a learning family, and the children quickly get a sense of the kind of rapport a teacher will develop with a class. After one candidate's lesson, a second-grader was taken aside and asked what he thought of that teacher. The boy identified parts of the lesson that he enjoyed, but said that it looked like the teacher had a hard time keeping the class calm. His opinion was that "if it's this bad now, it will probably be like that all the time." When asked for a final recommendation on this candidate, he said he thinks, "we should hold out for a better one."

A group of first- and second-grade students asked one teacher candidate about some aspects of teaching that they think are important, such as effective teaching: "How would you teach kids to read?" "If I had a hard time reading the chapter, what would you do?" "Do you know about draft books [process writing]?" "How do you teach math?"

They asked questions to consider how well the teacher would fit into Huntington Woods' way of doing things: "Would you sit with kids at lunch?"

"Have you ever taught before?"

"Which classroom would you like to be in? Which kids [grade levels] do you like?"

"Would it feel better to team teach or teach alone?"

"Do you like to have fun with kids?" To this, the candidate told about some activities she does with children. She described how she had played with some of her present students, spraying them with water from a hose on a hot day. The students laughed, and thought this was great.

They also asked about classroom management and the teacher's understanding of lead management concepts: "What would you do if one of the kids would not sit down for our family meeting? What would you say to them? Would you yell?"

"Have you ever yelled at kids?"

"What if somebody is running in the classroom?"

"What do you mean by self-evaluating?"

"What if kids were pushing to test you as a teacher?"

"What if kids were fighting?" When the teacher told what she would do if children were fighting, the students went on to explain our system of talking through problems.

They then asked, "If kids were pushing, and one fell, then the other helped him up, what would you do?" When the candidate answered that she would ask both kids to take a rest, the children said quite loudly, "NO!! They solved it!" They explained to her that if a child who pushed another one then helped that child get up, in effect he had apologized, and if the other accepted it, then the two had solved their problem themselves. No intervention from an adult was needed. We were very pleased to see from these interviews that students understand lead management very well.

Students' parents and other observers express appreciation of the system of lead management at Huntington Woods.

- One mother commented,
  No one can make anyone else do quality work. At Huntington Woods students are in a learning environment that utilizes lead management skills like motivation and encouragement rather than coercion. The students come to believe that those who manage them will treat them well and have their best interests in mind. I have seen this in action and I am very grateful for it.

- Beatrice Darling:
  They have taught us really effective things, like, the teacher is not the boss in the classroom. The teacher is a *part* of the classroom, and needs to be respected, but teachers look at the children like they are people, too. They all respect each other.

- Parent Kyle Martin:
  The atmosphere starts at the top, with the principal, spreads to the teachers, and to the students. The parents can't help but become caught up into it, because there is a great feeling of happiness and caring.

- A visitor wrote:
  Each child that we asked (during our visit) said that the teachers here "don't get mad at you" like teachers in other schools do. I think that speaks very convincingly that what you are doing is working, for everybody.

Chapter 6

SELF-EVALUATION

Evaluation for Students
Evaluation for Adults
Evaluation for the School

Chapter 6

SELF-EVALUATION

I have noticed that happy people are constantly evaluating themselves and unhappy people are constantly evaluating others.

--William Glasser (1996)

How do we teach children to work to a level of quality far beyond "good enough"? How can we help them achieve their very best performance? Individuals improve and grow the most when they self-assess. The ability to look at what one is doing and figure out how to improve it is a cornerstone not only of quality learning, but also of a successful life.

Evaluation for Students

Starting in the earliest grades, students at Huntington Woods learn to evaluate their own work for quality. One way we teach is by modeling the skills we want them to learn. Our team teaching format helps us to model evaluation for students, and we believe this is one of the most valuable things we do for them. It is important that students see us at times doing our highest quality work, going back and improving things, and talking them over with someone else, until we are really pleased with our performance. Often during lunch times, teachers tell children that they want to do some lesson planning during lunch. We sometimes have students ask if they may sit at the table with the teachers and listen in as they do their lesson design. This gives students the opportunity to see adults sharing ideas, talking them through to improve them, implementing them, and then evaluating them for continued improvement.

To teach self-evaluation directly, we begin very simply. The little children are asked to look at something they have done, such as a drawing, and think of one thing they can do to make it better. Since students are just learning self-evaluation, we do not always ask them actually to make the improvement in an assignment. Sometimes we just want them to do the thinking necessary for a good self-evaluation so that they can improve their performance next time.

They learn to rate their performance routinely as part of many activities. Their teachers ask them, for example, "Hold up your fingers and show us: when you worked together on this project just now, how well do you think your group did at getting along together?" The students hold up the number of fingers, from zero to ten, to rate themselves. They might be asked to rate "How well did your group do at keeping a reasonable noise level?" "How well did your group do at listening to different ideas? At supporting others' ideas?" We also list some criteria such as these for the children to use to self-evaluate with their groups, and give them time to discuss their evaluations together. As they begin to write, students rate themselves in writing, often by writing down the number from zero to ten that they think they rate for each criterion.

Young readers evaluate their reading progress by reading aloud and recording it on audio tape, then repeating after a couple of months. They listen to both tapes, comparing and evaluating their progress according to a rubric that their teachers discuss with them. Older students continue these methods of self-evaluation, and also do more revising of their work.

- Fourth- and fifth-grade students write weekly letters to their parents, in which they tell what they have learned, evaluate and write about what they did best in, and what they could improve, and then set a goal for themselves for the following week.

●Students work on projects in cooperative groups of two or three students, then follow up by writing about what went well in their groups, what they need to improve, and how well each person did his or her job.

Marilyn Spreng, who teaches lower-elementary children, said:

> To get the idea of quality across to these young children, the thing that has worked best for me is just to say, 'Is this your best work?' 'Is this the best that you can do now?' They'll be honest and say 'No.' Or if I know it's not their best, I might send it back and say, 'Would you please do one more thing to make it better, and bring it back and show me.' A little bit at a time now!
>
> We talk about when we need to do quality work and when we don't. If it is just a practice paper, you probably don't have to do quality writing. But if you are writing a letter, then your spelling should be correct and it should be your best work.

Teacher Ronda Pifer described how students learn self-evaluation:

> At first when students begin to evaluate, they try to say what the teacher wants them to say. A lot of times they will comment on something like, 'There could be more punctuation.' They might not even know what punctuation is, but they think that's a teacher kind of thing to say. 'There should be more punctuation and I should have written it neater'; that might be their first evaluation. Next it starts turning into, 'I think I could have written it neater, but I really didn't have a lot of time and I worked as best I could in the time I had.' And then down the road you hear, 'Here's my paper. This was the neatest I had time for, but if you let me keep it for one more hour, I can redo it, and it will be my very best.' So we see the depth of that change.

When we have a new fourth-grader or fifth-grader come into Huntington, they might be used to getting an 'A'. When they turn in a self-evaluation, they will say, 'This would be an 'A' in my old school.' We ask them what makes it an 'A'; 'Well, I did all the things I was supposed to do." We ask them some questions, and they start to think, but you can just see them holding on to the idea that, 'But it would be an 'A' someplace else.'

Even when fifth-graders come in with that pre-set concept of what an 'A' is, by the time they are at the end of fifth grade, they're able to see the difference between getting an 'A' and doing their best. One fifth-grader said that he thought an 'A' put a roof on things because you could only go so far. So when there's not an 'A', you just keep going and going and going.

Teaching assistant Paul Debri spoke about student self-evaluation:

I get to work with a few students on an individual basis with reading and writing. It is great to hear them self-evaluating. They are so proud that they are learning sets of word families, writing short stories, and reading better than they were a month or two ago. I hear 'I'm doing great!' 'I'm moving right along!' and 'I'm getting better!' I enjoy every minute I'm with them, and I enjoy it even more when they express their achievements.

For self-evaluation to be most meaningful, the person making the evaluation must understand the goal and agree with the criteria used to evaluate. This is part of thinking through the "What do I want?" question in the self-evaluation process. An important aspect of getting students to do quality work, therefore, is to teach them what 'quality work' means. We talk with our students often about the meaning of quality, and about how things could be improved. Teachers and students discuss these criteria, and also work together to develop *rubrics* and *checklists* to identify quality work and guide students' evaluations. Depending on the activity, the rubric may be developed by teachers, or students may be involved in developing it. Either way, teachers and students discuss it so that they agree on what it means and how to apply it. Our students then evaluate their own performance according to these standards.

One sample checklist is shown here:

Self-directed learner

Responsibility

I have a good school/work attendance record.
I meet school/work deadlines.
I demonstrate self-control where minimum directions and supervision are given.
I set goals.

Organization

I develop and follow a plan for completing a task.
I set high standards for quality and observe details needed to maintain it.
I read directions fully, take notes, and make calculations.
I seek information and research to find an answer.

Flexibility and initiative

I seek opportunities to learn new skills.
I observe, consider, and describe better ways to complete a task.
I maintain high performance standards without supervision.
I go beyond what is asked to improve my project.
I recognize a need or opportunity on my own and take appropriate actions.
I accept new or changed responsibilities.

Other categories for which this checklist gives guidelines include: Complex thinker, Effective citizen, Contributor to well being of the group, Cooperative worker, and Effective communicator.

Simply asking students always to do their best can be a trap. It is just as important to evaluate what we are giving the students to do, and to make that tough judgment call of whether or not it is worthy of their best efforts. One of the things that successful adults learn is the skill of judging when it is important to do things to the very best of one's ability, and when and in what kinds of activities to do just what is necessary. We need to help our students learn the difference.

We teach them that when they are writing something like a grocery list, or a note to themselves, it is not necessary to have terribly neat handwriting or accurate spelling. But when they are writing, for example, a letter to a company to complain about a product, or inquiring about employment, it is important that that letter is of high quality and clearly states their case. We believe that helping our students to differentiate the level of quality that is appropriate is just as important as teaching them that, for example, recreational reading can be done more quickly than technical reading.

Concurrent evaluation by teachers is used together with self-evaluation to give students and parents a complete picture of children's progress. Rather than relying on grades alone, we use several kinds of assessments to demonstrate students' mastery of subject matter. Oral and written projects, authentic assessments such as presentations to learning families and parents, portfolios, journals, standardized tests, tests composed by teachers, and tests devised by students are all employed.

- **Report cards**

Our report cards are still evolving. We have changed them each year, working to make them easy for the parents to read and understand, and to ensure that they keep good records--enough of the right kinds of information on students' progress and areas where they need help. We are working with parents to identify what all of us think is important for our children to know and be able to do at the end of the second grade and at the end of fifth grade, including the values that we teach. The report cards that we are currently using were designed with help from our students' parents. Each curriculum area is reported on one large sheet that lists standards for Early Childhood (kindergarten), first and second grades, or third, fourth, and fifth grades. The Language Arts sheet, for example, is divided in sections for Reading, Writing, Speaking, Listening, and Research, with the appropriate goals for each grade level; see the samples that follow.

LANGUAGE ARTS: Writing

Early Childhood:
- Write individually and in a group to communicate a message using the developmental stages of writing for a variety of purposes.
- Individually and in a group create a language experience and dictated stories for publication using prewriting strategies.

Grade 1:
- *Correctly spell in context high frequency use and frequently misspelled words appropriate for first grade.*
- Individually construct a complete sentence including a noun, a verb, capitalization and a punctuation mark using correct and legible printing.
- Write at least three related sentences based on a personal experience using legible printing.

Grade 2:
- Write a story with a title, middle and end using capitalization and ending punctuation using appropriate spacing and legible writing.
- Write and send a friendly letter to a person; include date, greeting, content-focused body, closing and name using legible writing.
- *Correctly spell in context high frequency and frequently misspelled words appropriate to second grade.*
-

Memory learning goals are printed in italics, with a note that memorizing is most effective when done individually with parent help. Each goal is scored with one of:

P--practiced but has not yet demonstrated standard requirements
1--demonstrated some standard requirements, several errors (60% to 79%)
2--demonstrated standard requirements, few errors (80% to 89%)
3--exceeds all standard requirements, minimal errors (90% and above).

LANGUAGE ARTS: Writing

Grade 3:
- *Correctly spell in context high frequency use and frequently misspelled words appropriate for third grade.*
- Legibly write in print and cursive.
- Write narrative and persuasive paragraphs using a topic sentence, supporting details and a conclusion relating to a personal experience.
- Write an expository report based upon a topic of interest. Use writing process strategies and focus on prewriting and draft.

Grade 4:
- Use legible handwriting or word processing to compose a letter of request, and invitation and a thank-you.
- Write expository and persuasive paragraphs organizing and analyzing information focusing on process writing skills (brainstorming, drafting, feedback, revising, editing and publishing).
- Individually or in a group, create a Reader's Theater with main and supporting characters. Use process writing and focus on exaggerations.
- *Correctly spell in context high frequency use and frequently misspelled words appropriate for fourth grade.*

Grade 5:
- Write a conversation focusing on characterization using quotation marks to show dialogue and apostrophes to show possession.
- Process write (brainstorm, first draft, feedback, revise, edit, final copy, and publish) a description focusing on sensory words and organization. Use a thesaurus for more vivid and varied language.
- *Spell in context high frequency use and frequently misspelled words appropriate for fifth grade.*
- Write technical text to accomplish a task (ex. Directions for a game) with multiple steps or directions. Evaluate the completion of the task by a peer.
- Write paragraphs to create an historical fiction composition containing correct use of present, past, or future tense verbs.

- **Narrative evaluations**

The older students are involved in marking their own report cards. They also write narrative self-evaluations that go along with the report card each reporting period, then meet with their teachers in order to reach consensus on the student and teacher evaluations. In the narrative self-evaluations, students look at each subject area in school, as well as the school rules, and write for their parents what they have learned, how they think they have performed in each area, and what they could do to improve. They set a goal, and in the narrative they ask their parents for any help that they might need to reach it.

Learning families develop guidelines for the students to use in writing their narratives. Here is an example from one upper elementary learning family:

Student Narrative

Useful Learning (Choose two of the following four questions.)

1. How is what you are learning at Huntington Woods going to help you in your life?
2. Describe some areas where you have done quality work.
3. Where do you need help or where would you like to improve?
4. What can your parents do to help you? What can your teachers do to help you?

Warm and Supportive Environment (Please write about each of the following questions.)

*1. How do you help Huntington Woods' warm and caring environment? What could you do better to help the environment? (Include the four school rules)
*2. How do you know others care for you and what are you doing to show you care?

Self-Evaluation
*1. What is the best part of self-evaluation? What is the hardest part of self-evaluation?

A student in the fifth grade in another learning family, using a different set of guidelines, wrote this narrative:

Dear Reader,
This is my year end evaluation. In it you will see how I have improved, areas I have done well in, areas I need to improve in, and my feelings about this year.

READING
In reading I have increased my vocabulary, and learned to challenge myself better. I have improved at reading to people when I had to read part of my book to the teacher. My favorite book I read this year was *Jurassic Park* by Michael Crichton. My favorite category is horror. I have always enjoyed reading, but now I like it even better.

HISTORY
I learned a lot about history this year. I learned about Native Americans, miners, pioneers, and lumberjacks. I also learned about Michigan's past like when the capitol moved to Lansing from Detroit, and when people first settled in Michigan and made Michigan a state. Before I never did much work in history, but this year I learned a lot. History isn't my favorite subject, but I still like it.

MATH
Math is my favorite subject. I feel that I do very well in math. I like doing fractions, decimals, and percents. I can multiply and divide them all. I can also do long division. I am in the discovery math group. That is the group of kids who are excelling in math. I joined late, but I caught up easily. Next year I will be in 7th grade math and English. Next year I want to learn more about square root.

WRITING
I love writing stories. I wrote three stories over four pages each. One of them was seven pages. I do most of my writing work on the computer to help prepare me for the future. I like to write fiction stories, but if I was assigned to write a non-fiction I could.

QUALITY
I like doing quality work. Quality means trying your best and always trying to improve. Just because I am going to a different school doesn't mean I will stop doing quality work. I hope to have a good year in Jr. high next year.

WORKING WITH OTHERS
I feel that I have worked well with others this year. I just came this year and I made many friends. I work well with my group members and help them with things like spelling, Math, etc. And sometimes they help me.

136

After writing their self-evaluations, students receive narrative evaluations from their teachers. For example, one team of teachers wrote this year-end letter to another student, Jesse:

Last year we remember writing 'short and sweet' at the beginning of our narrative. This year we'd like to do the same thing. Your narrative was brief and to the point. You do so much excellent work that for some reason you just don't take credit for. Why is that? You also have some areas to improve that you don't even mention. Your narrative is a place to brag about your strengths, and ask for help to overcome your weaknesses. We hope that you communicate both strengths and weaknesses when you talk to your parents.

We agree that you are a great reader. We like to see you get excited about the *Narnia* series by C.S. Lewis. Those are not easy books, and yet you are flying right through them. You are also getting better at math this year as the year goes along. Are those the only things that you do well in school? They are the only things that you wrote about. What about Central Study? You got into the election '96 unit so deeply that you wanted to hold an election for class president, and then run for the position! How are you doing on your ILS lessons? You have passed all of the fifth-grade lessons, and are half way through the eighth-grade work. Do your parents know about that? That is something you should celebrate!

You wrote that you need to improve your Spanish. What else can you improve? Do you study your spelling words every week? You have done well in spelling, but not as well as you could if you studied. How about writing? You have written a couple of stories this year. Were they the best you could make them? Are you a good listener? Do you challenge yourself? Do you settle for getting finished? Is 'good enough' good enough for you? These are questions that we reserve for students who are doing very well in school when compared to others, but not so well when compared to themselves. You have such a high level of skills, Jesse, but you don't always use them to do high quality work. At Huntington Woods, the only limits on what you can do are the limits that you place on yourself. You are beginning to limit yourself.

What do we mean by that? Well, we see you start things and not finish them. For example, the school-wide TV news was a great idea that you had, but you only did it once. Designing and teaching a lesson in class was a great idea that you never pursued. Holding a classroom debate is a great idea that you don't seem to want to follow through with. Assembling a jury of your peers is a fantastic idea that you brought up early in the year and haven't mentioned since.

Does it seem like we're picking on you? We're not. We love you, and want to challenge you to get out of your 'comfort zone.' Right now you are comfortably doing what it takes to get by, but you are cheating yourself of some great learning and some fun times at Huntington Woods. We know that you want to do more, deep in your heart. Step up to the plate and take your best swing! Try something new! All big hitters hit many home runs, but they strike out much more often. If one of your ideas strikes out, you have others to try…

In reply, Jesse wrote:

Just a little memo:

I'm just going to answer the questions that you put on my narrative. The main reason I don't make my narratives real long or even average is because I don't like to brag and I don't see all the quality work that I do. I see it as just another ordinary thing I do and you see it as something that is out of the ordinary. The way I interpreted what you wanted me to write about my strengths is that you wanted me to write my main strength. I also thought the same way about my weaknesses. There are some cases where good enough is good enough for me but when we come back from intersession you will see a different, better for understanding Me, but I'll talk to you later about that. I'm making a pact to myself to always challenge myself. By the way what is my 'comfort zone'?

Our students' parents tell us that they like the narrative reporting we have developed. While a few parents ask for letter

138

grades, most say they prefer to have the specific summaries of what their child has learned and where he or she needs more work.

- **Student-led conferences**

[Students can do a good job evaluating and showing growth] only if we do a good enough job in teaching them how to select, reflect and set goals...They need to know what they know. They need to know that other skills are possible goals in order to make informed decisions for where to go next in their learning. And they will only learn this if we teach them to think about their learning in a critical, reflective manner.

--Cheryl H. Jonsson. 1993 (page 21)

Students report their progress to their parents at conferences they lead themselves. In these conferences, they tell about projects of which they are particularly proud and that they believe evidence quality work, and also discuss some areas in which they are working toward improvement. They show parents their portfolios, which contain samples of their work in different subject areas. By preparing to present their work in this way, students learn to reflect and state what they are learning in each sample.

At one conference time, Mandy, a lower-elementary girl, conducted a conference with her parents. She had practiced the things she wanted to say with an older student earlier in the week, so she felt quite confident and well prepared. She had written out an agenda listing the things that she wanted to show her parents. Each time she explained one of the items, she would look back at the agenda and check off the item. After she finished each segment of her conference, she said to her parents, "Do you have any questions before we move on to the next topic?"

Her composure while leading the conference very much impressed her mother and father, who listened with attention while Mandy went through each subject area and showed them her work. She had examples ready of assignments and projects in each subject area. She told about the steps of process writing, and read to her parents from some of the writing she had published. She talked about the things she does well and also about the things she would like to improve, mentioning things she planned to try.

After parents confer with children and their teachers, we invite their feedback with a survey like this one:

POST CONFERENCE PARENT SURVEY

Dear Parents,

It was exciting to see the enthusiasm students put into learning how to assess themselves and their own work as they prepared for our student led parent teacher conferences. This process allowed them a true sense of ownership as they were given the opportunity to evaluate their own progress and discuss their findings with you.

It is very important to all of us at HW to have you share some feedback about this conferencing format. It will be helpful in planning future conferences of this nature.

1. Did you feel this was a valuable experience for you as parents?
2. Was a reasonable amount of time allowed to accommodate your needs?
3. Do you feel that your child felt more ownership in her/his work and evaluation by using this process?
4. Do you have any suggestions for improvement of future student led conferences?

Parents make comments such as these on the surveys:

- Yes, [the student-led conference was valuable in that] I was able to see my child enjoy her accomplishments and recognize areas for improvement. The time allowed was great. It gave freedom to sit and listen without feeling rushed.

- I liked the idea of your class practicing with older students. It showed itself by my child going through her work and explaining things in a very organized manner.

We also ask parents to provide feedback to their children after student-led conferences.

POST CONFERENCE PARENT REFLECTIONS

Dear parents,
Please write a letter to your son or daughter reflecting on the conference. Some items you may want to include are listed below. Please return this letter as soon as possible. Thank you once again for choosing to take an active role in your child's education. Your participation reinforces to your child that his/her education is important; not only to you, but for his/her future. Please keep in mind that this is a personal letter to your child, and I will be reading it only if she or he chooses to ask me to.

- What has made you feel proud?
- You would like to have your child work on...
- I know that sometimes you have difficulty..., but...
- I am glad to see that you are taking an active role in your own education...
- I am glad to see that you are making an extra effort in...

Mandy's parents wrote her this post-conference letter:

Dear Mandy,
Your Dad and I are so very proud of how well you're doing in school. We can hardly believe you're reading third grade books and you are only a first grader. That's super!
The stories that you have written are just great. If you keep learning all of your spelling words like you have been, pretty soon you'll know how to write and spell all of the words.

I was glad to see you doing such a good job with your Student-Led Conference. I can tell you are proud of all your schoolwork.

> Love,
> Mom and Dad

A few other examples of letters parents wrote to their children are these:

- Dustin,
  You did a great job at school this last quarter. Keep up the good work, especially on your stories. We are glad that you are making an extra effort to help Nick learn to read better. We know that sometimes you have difficulty with your class work but keep trying your best. We would like to have you work a little harder at being a self-directed student. We are glad that you are taking an active role in your education. Keep up the good work. Your improvement in your behavior and helping others makes us very proud of you.
  Great job!

  > Love you,
  > Mom and Dad

- Dear Alyssa,
  We were so happy to see your quality work at your conference! We were proud of your work, and very proud that you are reading so well!
  We know that sometimes it is hard for you to finish your work because you like to talk to your friends, but we can see that you are trying to do better. We like to see finished work!
  Keep up the good work in reading and writing—you're doing a great job!

  > Love,
  > Mom and Dad

- Dear Adam,
  I'm so proud of you. Your conference was great! I'm especially proud of your report card, and Daddy will be, too. I see you can be serious when you want to be. We know you can do it when you put your mind to it. So let's keep it up, ok?

I would like to see you work more on keeping focused on all your schoolwork. See if you can get all 3's on the next report card.

Keep up the good work on your spelling and reading. I know how hard you work. The more you read and spell, the better you will be. We know sometimes you have difficulty in paying attention, but as we keep saying to you, it's very important to have good grades in school.

I'm proud to see that you take responsibility for your actions. That means you're growing up. We're glad to see that you make a real effort to try to act real good in class. Keep up the good work, Adam, and it will pay off one day.

Love,
Mom and Dad

Our students' parents express confidence that self-evaluation is worthwhile:

- My son is learning to evaluate his own work. During the year...he takes time, he looks over what he has done to see if it's good, and then, when it comes up to conference time, he shows us where he started and where he is now. It's really neat; he can see the advance from where he started out to where he is. When he sees how he's advancing it gives him the ability to keep going. When I heard that the students here were going to do their own evaluations, I really didn't have too much doubt about its value, because I figured that if these kids are going to be involved in making their own judgments, then they're going to improve. If I evaluate my own job, the way I do things, I feel proud when I see what I can do. If I don't evaluate my job, I'll get stagnant, and then I don't advance. I don't improve the quality. It's the same for the kids.

- The self-evaluations that the students do are an excellent way to reinforce the positive that a child has learned, but leaves them room for growth. It also provides them the training to self-evaluate, which is very much a part of the real 'work' world.

One student said,

- I do self-evaluating by doing things like evaluating how I did and what I need to improve on some of the work I have done. I use a rubric by checking off the things I have done and leaving blank the things I need to do; then I go back and do them. Self-evaluating is hard. When you have to think of what you need to do to improve, sometimes it takes a while.

A visitor to Huntington Woods wrote:

- (Students') self-assessment was amazing. They understood what they were supposed to do and how they were expected to do it, which isn't that unusual. But they were able to articulate the amount of effort they were putting forth and how it was resulting in improved performance...Self-evaluating children will not remain average. They will get better and better, because they are learning to demand it of themselves.

Evaluation for Adults

At Huntington Woods, all of us on the staff are constantly self-evaluating and making changes. In our lead-managed system, instructional paraprofessionals, secretary, and custodians use self-evaluation rather than being evaluated by a supervisor. Each establishes a goal that he or she would like to pursue during the year. The employee lets the principal know if any help is wanted to achieve it, and evaluates the success of his or her own efforts.

With lead management, in an atmosphere of trust and professionalism, teachers are best able to identify areas for their own improvement. Tenured teachers write a goal for improvement for the year, and then let Kaye know if they would like help in reaching that goal. Here are a few examples of goals teachers set for themselves:

- This year will prove to be an exciting and interesting one. I am looking forward to the new knowledge that I will gain this year. I hope to improve my skills in many areas. I am pleased to work with two fantastic teachers. My goal this year is to implement the 'Literacy for Learning' program that I was trained in. There are many facets to the program. I plan to begin implementation slowly. I want to begin with draft books. I picture students writing page after page, and being very excited about it. I will look at the draft books to measure individual student learning and plan what to teach next. My lessons will be driven by student need and not by a plan book written three weeks in advance. I anticipate a few problems in the beginning. Until I work out a system it will seem a bit overwhelming to look at each draft book every night. However, because I so strongly believe in the program I will make it work. The heart of the 'Literacy for Learning' program is driven by the cycle of ASSESSMENT - EVALUATION - PLANNING - and TEACHING.

I will know that I have succeeded in my goal by looking at student progress. The writing and reading skills in EVERY child should be greatly increased. Student attitude will also be a terrific measure. Lessons will be so individualized that students should not feel a great deal of the frustration that can accompany new learning. The lessons will be totally relevant and useful.

- I will work on achieving the following goals throughout the 1996-1997 school year:

  1. I will get to know at least one special hobby or interest that each student in our Learning Family possesses.
  2. I will continue to use Reality Therapy/Choice Theory, and teach and model it to our students.
  3. I will design curricular projects for students integrating activities to meet the five basic needs.
  4. I will work on knowing better the individual academic needs of students in our math group by working with small skill groups.

- My first goal for this school year is to strive for and maintain a consistent learning environment in my classroom that meets the students' picture of a quality family. To do this I need to work on maintaining my voice level, implement more ideas to satisfy my students' need for fun of through the use of music, energizers, and activities, enrich use of self-evaluation with constant modeling, increase the use of student-generated rubrics and product demonstrations, and continually provide opportunities to strengthen cooperative unity. I will be able to monitor my improvement in these areas by observing the interaction of the students in the classroom and receiving feedback from the students and my peers.

My second goal is to implement the teaching of the eight values embraced by Huntington Woods. I will achieve this by discussion during family meetings, role-plays with the students, student observation, modeling, and activities designed to promote awareness and learning. These values will be assessed using student-created rubrics along with teacher judgment.

My third and final goal for this school year is to complete work on the curriculum for Huntington Woods by designing rubrics for the Language Arts standards.

Midway through the year, the principal follows up on the plans by writing a note to each teacher, asking how he or she is doing on progress toward the goal, as a reminder to self-evaluate. It is up to each teacher to select his or her goal, decide what to do to accomplish it, and assess how well he or she has succeeded.

For probationary teachers, who need evaluation forms completed for the school district, supervisor evaluation is used concurrently with self-evaluation. Kent Snoeyink describes how it works:

As a probationary teacher for my first four years, I needed to be evaluated by the principal. Kaye, of course, has me *self* evaluate. At a time that's convenient for me, she sits in on a lesson and scripts out everything that happens, each thing that I say and that students say. Then she hands me the district's teacher evaluation forms and has me fill them out about myself, using information in the script. I give those filled-out forms to Kaye. She looks them over, and then sets up a conference with me. We then discuss the lesson, the good points about it, and the parts that I need to spend time fixing. Lead management at its best!

After the two have gone over the evaluation together, the principal signs the district evaluation forms and sends them in.

As the leader, the principal also establishes goals for improvement, and evaluates her progress toward those goals. To model self-evaluation for teachers and other employees, she shares her goals with them and, periodically throughout the year, talks with them about how she is doing on accomplishing the goals that she has set. Some sample entries from Huntington's first year follow:

- In retrospect, what a wonderful week! We got some great plans decided for Intersession—I think kids will love it. Spanish is working, the computer lab is working, choice time is working. Tulip bulb planting was great. Team training for parents was extremely well received. Teachers seem to be overcoming some frustrations, and each day goes better.

- I can't believe how lax I've been in keeping up with journal writing! I did better when we were all doing it as a group. Last week was a great week—I was really glad to see all the kids and teachers [after an out of town trip].
  I had a call from Ronda last night. It got me thinking about the whole curriculum issue—the importance of being purposeful, teaching for mastery, etc.

- This past week really flew by—there's so much good stuff going on here! Four [parent] action teams met this week. They're functioning very well. New students starting Monday, and what a great feeling to be proud of everything we saw [when showing them around] and not have to worry about what we *might* see. Students are really able to articulate what goes on at this school.
  Good staff meeting yesterday discussing decision-making model and ways to find time to counsel students. [Staff members] brainstormed great suggestions and were very helpful to each other.

Kaye has periodically shared her weekly journal with teachers. After reading it, one wrote in reply (in part),

> Everything at HW is so much better than in August. It's good to look back in the journals to see how far we've come! I also like the feeling around school that once we get a program going or solve a problem, we are on to working on improving another aspect here—constant improvement.
>
> It's also fun to see you around school this year. You're smiling more and are less in a hurry.

These are some remarks teachers share about self-evaluation:

- As a team, we use self-evaluation daily. Every day, we go over the day and find areas where we could improve. Especially in management techniques, and lesson design-- ways that it could have been more effective for the students. Personally, I use self-evaluation not only as a teacher, but also in my life on a day-to-day basis, asking myself, 'How can I improve?' Quality is never static, and it is important for me as a teacher in school and as a person out of school to improve constantly.

- Each day I go home thinking, 'Okay, next time I will definitely do this...' or 'Boy, that really worked well!' [My co-teacher and I] talk before we go home: 'Is there anything you want to change?' 'Do you want to try something else?' We are always trying to make it come out better...too many times, I think, we ask children to do their best work and then give them something that is not *our* best work. I don't feel good about doing that...They are asked to do quality [work]. Well, what about the adults in their life? Are they giving quality? I think everybody here is really striving for quality.

- Self-evaluation helps me stay very honest. It takes a very open approach, too. You can't be guarding your own ego or trying to build yourself up in the eyes of your colleagues at the expense of the students.

148

- **Self-evaluation in action: Friday Journal**

Team teaching in multi-age classrooms was a new experience for almost all of Huntington Woods' teachers during our first year in operation. The weekly journal kept by Andrea van der Laan reflects her thinking while integrating these major changes. Andrea had set a professional goal of improving her classroom management skills, and she used her journal to self-evaluate and think through what she was learning. Here are just a few of the entries, some of which are written as notes to the principal:

- I talked to Kaye Tuesday about problems with our team. Her suggestions were to start an agenda, also decide what will be done if a job isn't completed. I filled one out and showed Sandy and Sharon. It went over well. Two suggestions from Kaye--dole out jobs and teaching assignments.
  We got through the agenda. We also doled out jobs. We even had fun for a change during planning. We need to ask who's teaching what on Monday morning.
  I hope things start smoothing out soon. Plans seem to be going smoother--now let's work on our team.

- Kaye,
  This is the middle of the week, but I had to tell you about a 'teachable moment.'
  My class was talking about communication with one another when one of my students (Z.) complained about B. He said that he would tell B. to 'Stop it!' and B. would always come back with a nasty comment. This led into the [Choice] theory needs. We quickly reviewed the needs and I asked which need they thought B. was covering up by acting out. We finally decided (after brainstorming) that B. feels he may have a bad reputation and he doesn't belong. He's defensive because that way no one else can hurt him inside. It is a defense mechanism.
  My students agreed that we needed to help change his sense of belonging. After much discussion, it was decided that he should be invited to eat with a group of boys and also

learn a new card game with them. We discussed that B. would not be easy and this might take several weeks. This might be the toughest job they've ever had! I had five or six boys <u>volunteer</u> to try to make it work. They have already asked B. to join them for lunch.

The lesson went even farther than this. Some of my girls decided that C. and J. might need the same thing! It was their idea to work with them. I can't tell you how <u>delighted</u> I am with my class!

I've alerted Sharon as to our plans. B. is her case study (J. is mine). This might be a good time for some observation.

(Kaye Mentley replied,
WONDERFUL!! Well worth a Wednesday entry!)

- In at 7:15 - I got a lot done--what a great day. Our students worked so well, I took pictures! Z. told me he was removing <u>himself</u> because he was angry--that's a first.

   Mrs. U. visited the computer lab--Mrs. B. ate lunch with us today. Both [parents] seemed positive!

   Question: How do you keep 20 students on track when 3 or 4 are constantly doing their own thing?...We had a family meeting today, and it worked better. Z. was into Folktales, T. and M. worked cooperatively. I'm still working with M.--I'm not sure if I can get him back on task. Maybe after the sugar cube houses are done...

- Collaborative time, planning, paper work, grades have all fallen into place--A new focus this week would be Whisper Zones--Sometimes it works, sometimes it doesn't--What I have to remember is that my students react in direct conjunction to me - When I'm loud, they're loud. When I'm relaxed, they're relaxed. I need to refocus on my goals to lower my voice level. I'm not consistent. Most of the time I do well. I'm working on this aspect along with my students.

Now, in her fourth year at Huntington Woods, Andrea still writes in her Friday Journal.

Self-evaluation for the School

Self-evaluation is just as useful a tool for the school as a whole as it is for individuals, learning families, and teaching teams. As a staff, we want to know whether the things we do are working to achieve our goals, and what we might do that would work more effectively. Our collaborative planning meetings regularly include time to self-evaluate. We look at several kinds of information to develop a complete picture.

Assessments of student learning are one indicator. The Michigan Education Assessment Program (MEAP) is given to all our students, fourth graders being tested in math and reading. Our students' scores consistently exceed state averages.

- In 1996, reading levels of "satisfactory" or higher were achieved by 49.5% of students in the state, 52.3% in the district, and 88.2% at Huntington Woods.
- In math, 60.5% achieved or surpassed a satisfactory score statewide, 81.8% in our district, and 85.3% at HW.

We take into account that these scores reflect our whole population, including students who, at other schools, would be classified as variously disabled and impaired. Since we include all students in the learning families at our school, almost all of our students take this assessment. Only those very few whose parents request it are exempted.

Standardized reading assessments are used, which show that almost all students here are reading with comprehension at grade level or above. As explained in the section on the Reading Intervention program (in Chapter 7), we have developed the program to help those who read below grade level to develop their skills more fully.

Another way we monitor student success is to follow up when our students go on to middle school. We collect copies of our former students' report cards, and they show very high marks (summarized in the graphs below). One of the two district middle schools offers an advanced math class for sixth grade students. Of our twelve former students at that school, eight are enrolled in advanced math.

6th Grade Report Cards - '95-96

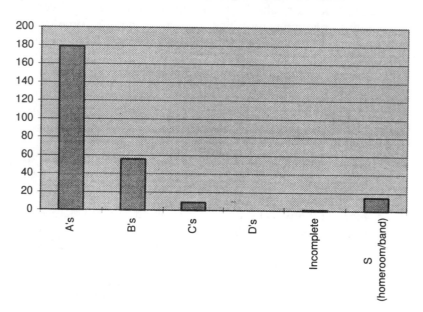

During the marking period shown on this chart, there were forty-seven former Huntington Woods students in sixth grade at the two district middle schools. Thirty-six report cards were returned for study.

In band and homeroom, students were sometimes given S [Satisfactory] or U [Unsatisfactory] rather than a letter grade.

6th Grade Report Cards - '96-97

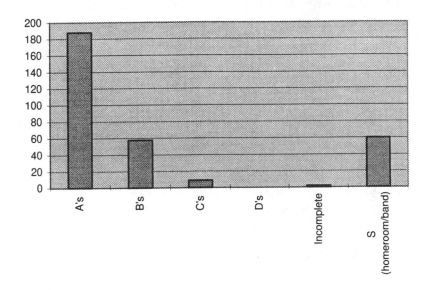

The transition from elementary to middle school is smooth for almost all students. Academically they do wonderfully. Emotionally, some of them find that they have to adjust somewhat. One former student said that the thing she missed most was the feeling she had at Huntington Woods that everybody loved her. She did not have that same feeling at her new school. Others have commented that they miss working in groups, saying that they think this is a better way to learn than working alone. Some also say that they miss tutoring younger children. Twenty to twenty-five of our former students come to Huntington on Wednesday mornings (during their schools' collaborative planning time) to visit, see friends, and tutor or otherwise help the teachers.

Parents have told us that the teachers at schools to which their children transfer have remarked on the students' good self-esteem.

The parents attribute that strength to their children's experience at Huntington Woods.

The opinions of educators, the public, and parents in our area indicate that they see Huntington Woods as successful. Several journals and newspapers have published articles about our school, and we receive many invitations to present HW at professional conferences and workshops. Our first annual Quality School Conference in April 1997 was filled to capacity, and feedback from those attending was overwhelmingly positive. Interest is high for the second conference. (For information about attending this daylong event, contact the school directly. The address is listed in *References and Resources.*)

Visitors come to see our school in person in greater numbers each year, over 900 in 1996-97. Many are experienced teachers and administrators, and their comments help us evaluate our programs. Here are some examples of visitor feedback which indicate that our programs are working effectively.

- The five of us who visited your school have spread the word of your program to everyone who will listen. We all agreed that it was one of the most enjoyable and motivating experiences in our education careers. Those that are lucky enough to spend their elementary years with you will develop socially, emotionally, and intellectually into the types of individuals we want and need to lead us in the future. We all know that what works best for your school won't necessarily work in another. You have motivated us, however, to look at what we do and ask ourselves if there is a better way. Thanks!

- I have remembered Dr. Glasser's work since reading *Schools Without Failure* way back in my undergraduate days. At the school where I teach, I sometimes hear the comment that since Dr. Glasser is not really a teacher, what he says probably won't work in schools. I am so pleased to be here and to see the Quality School ideas in action. I have talked to students and teachers, and it is apparent to me that this is a Quality School and it really is working.

- State Superintendent Robert Schiller said that his visit to Huntington Woods was 'one of the finest school visits of my career, because I saw things happen in that environment that foster innovations in education. As wonderful as this presentation is, you have to be there and experience it. This is a shining light in Michigan and in the nation of what we want education to be.'

We receive many applications from teachers who would like to join our faculty. Our relationship with the local teachers' union is very good. Seeing that the interests and professional goals of our staff members are well-served, the union has been very cooperative in helping us organize some of the changes we have made, such as altering the weekly schedule. The Wyoming Public Schools District Superintendent, Board members, and administrators consistently affirm and support our work at Huntington.

Our enrollment has increased by one hundred students since the school opened in 1993. As Huntington Woods is a School of Choice, families from our school district have first right to send their children here, with the remaining spaces then filled by a lottery of other applicants. Currently, 28 students from outside our district are enrolled, bringing increased revenue of more than $150,000 to the district. We think it significant that Wyoming Public Schools district employees and their relatives are enrolling their children at HW in increasing numbers, some families even moving so their children can attend.

Full inclusion in the learning families is succeeding very well. For the last three years as we have worked to eliminate special education, of the 700 students we have had in school, we have been able to maintain full time in general education all but two children.

Our students and staff members love to be here. It truly is a joyful place! This is one indicator that we are achieving the conditions for quality. The atmosphere in our school is lively, cheerful, and friendly. This is often noticed and commented on by people who come in for various reasons. The school's budget for repairing vandalism is zero, and the amount of actual damage is zero or very close to it each year.

Occasionally a child might write on a restroom wall or something of that sort. The few times this has occurred, other students immediately tell a teacher or the custodian, or simply get cleaning supplies and clean off the marks on their own.

Parents of our students are wonderfully supportive, to the extent that they donate an average of two hundred hours of volunteer time each week. (See Chapter 8 for a discussion of things we do to promote this involvement.) Some families who had moved out of the Wyoming area and removed their children from HW have returned specifically so that their children can attend school here. One father said, "I am *so* happy that we made up our minds to move back into the district. Now that our daughter has returned to Huntington, we have our bright, happy child back again."

One family who had moved because of a house fire has now returned to the Wyoming district, and three of their children are back at Huntington Woods after attending another school for six months. At school one day, Kaye asked the three to show with a quick 'finger vote' whether they were glad to be back, on a scale of one to ten with ten fingers to indicate 'super glad' and zero for 'not glad at all.' She said later, 'All three immediately held up 'ten,' and their faces were just beaming.'

She talked a little longer with the oldest boy, Chris, who had just finished the fourth grade at the other school. 'I'd like to ask you for some more votes, Chris. You were all done with school for the summer, but now, being back here, you have school until July 28th. Do you still want to come to school until the end?' she asked. He quickly held up ten fingers. 'Do you want to come to Intersession this summer?' Chris flashed 'ten' again.

When she asked, 'What did you notice that was different at the other school?' Chris answered, "They didn't seem like they loved me like people do here. Another thing was that they gave us treats. If I always did my homework, or when I got the words all right on my spelling test, I got a treat.' Kaye said, 'Did getting the treats make you a better speller?' 'Not really,' was the reply. When she added, 'You know you won't be getting treats now, because we don't do that here at Huntington,' Chris said, 'I guess not. We don't need it here.'

(above) Labeled storage shelves help children learn
       organization skills.
Students are interested in learning to read when they can write
their own stories. Adults help by writing down sentences the
students dictate (below).

Once students can read independently, they are found reading all over the school - in the corridor (above) - and outdoors (below).

Working together helps everyone to learn.

Older students tutor younger ones (above), and table groups form cooperative learning teams (below).

Useful learning can employ both high technology and low-tech tools.

Students show their parents the things they have been
learning in conferences they conduct themselves.

Parents are very active participants in the Huntington Woods community, forming close bonds between learning families in school and families at home. Parent volunteers do everything from helping tutor students (above) to assembling our playground equipment (below).

The practice of self-evaluation keeps us open to new possibilities that will help us move toward our goals as individual staff members and students, and as a whole system. One visitor to Huntington Woods commented,

> I have visited the school several times now, over three years. Each time I come here, I observe things that they do differently, that have been changed to work better. I can see that the people at this school really do believe in continual self-evaluation for improvement.

Chapter 7

QUALITY LEARNING

Homework
Learning Family Play
Community Service as Useful Learning:
    Casey's Restaurant
Teaching Reading
Using Technology instead of Textbooks
Learning Choice Theory

Chapter 7

QUALITY LEARNING

Education is the process through which we discover that learning adds quality to our lives. Until this happens, students have little incentive to learn anything more than they already know...If [students whom you are trying to teach] are learning a great deal, you can be certain that what they are learning is adding quality to their lives. If they are having difficulty learning, you can be equally certain that what you are trying to teach them is not adding quality to their lives.

-- William Glasser (in Greene, 1989)

What kind of teaching and learning help children become so enthusiastic that they ask their parents things like, "Can we come home from our vacation by Saturday? Our school is having the Civil War reenactment day, and I want to be there when it starts at 5am"?

Students in our Quality School are not asked to do the low-quality learning of "throwaway knowledge," memorizing information that is irrelevant to their lives, and must be learned only to pass a test (for example, memorizing dates and places of battles as a way to study history). Instead, thematic interdisciplinary units demonstrate to students the connections between all subject areas. Teachers plan hands-on projects that help to make lessons meaningful.

As William Glasser has written in *Schools Without Failure* (1969, page 30),

> We cannot assume that children know why they are in school, that they understand the value of education and its application to them. From kindergarten through graduate school, we must teach students, or help them discover for themselves, the relationship of what they are learning to their lives.

Current research, Thomas Armstrong writes,

> ...suggests that all students benefit more from project-based environments in which they actively construct new meanings based upon their existing knowledge of a subject. That means that...students need to be questioning, hypothesizing, experimenting, interviewing, collaborating, problem-solving, and more.
>
> (1995, page 54)

Our students think this kind of learning makes a lot of sense for them. One girl, Paula, said:

> I like working in groups and solving problems hands-on. It's easier when you can see what you are working on, not just listen to the teacher explaining it.

Hands-on activities are the way into students' hearts and into their minds. Some of the activities that we do are creating models of different kinds, drawing, painting, and sculpting. Students sculpt with peanut butter, modeling materials, and *papier mache*. They make their own manipulative objects for math and language lessons. We get them to build things, do role plays and drama, and go on field trips, to excite students' interest and channel their energy in a creative way. When students are engaged, they are happy, and present no discipline problems.

Activities involving movement can be used to review content, discharge restless energy, build group cohesion, and have a little fun. Teachers often use 'energizers' in the learning families. One example, Musical Circles, begins with everyone standing. When students hear the music begin to play, they walk (or dance) around the room. When it stops, everyone freezes in place, looking at the teacher. The teacher holds up one hand, with fingers showing the number of students she or he would like in each group. While still holding her hand in the air, she gives the students the topic to discuss. When she drops her hand to her side, that is the signal to students to move into the groups with the students nearest them and discuss the topic. When the music starts again, the children start moving again. If the Musical Circles activity is being used to review content, the topics for discussion are material from the lesson. The activity might also be used with questions to help students get to know each other better. (Mentley, 1997)

Teachers might also have children form a large circle, then throw a soft rubber 'Koosh' ball to each in turn. The student holding the ball asks a question for the others to answer, then tosses it to someone else. These are all fun ways to involve students. With good planning, students can be active and enjoy their time in school. While learning the curriculum by using all the mental, physical, and emotional ways of knowing available to them, they also learn cooperation and interaction skills.

Homework

Research shows that when schools routinely require students to do homework assignments, it does not have a positive effect on learning. We also have learned that having compulsory homework can cause tension between parents and their children, between parents and teachers, and students and teachers.

There is often a great deal of nagging, bribing and threatening by adults to try to compel students to complete mandatory homework. When students do not finish assigned homework, even the warmest and least coercive teachers believe that they have no choice but to punish with failing grades or loss of privileges. Even the best students, who do their homework, resent the fact that their teacher will punish them if they stop doing it. Compulsion of any kind undermines the non-coercive environment we work to achieve, and even students who will do homework do not do high quality work on assignments of this kind. They do just enough to get by, so homework becomes the enemy of quality.

Because Huntington Woods is founded on the philosophy of Quality Schools, students are asked to do only useful work that is relevant to their lives, and therefore we focus on the skills of reading, writing and problem solving. We think that the very best things that parents can do with their children after school, rather than helping with homework, are reading to them, talking with them, and perhaps teaching them a new hobby or activity that child and parent can do together.

Homework is used as a supplement to class work, designed to extend learning and stimulate interest in the topics being taught. If students do not finish things in class, they may be asked to complete them at home. There are also some learning activities that can best be done at home. For example, while an upper elementary learning family studied students' family trees in a unit on history, students interviewed older family members about family relationships and collected photographs of themselves and their relatives. These materials were then used in class to construct paint and collage representations of family trees on paper, and to do writing activities about their family histories. The unit linked with other learning about historic events in the country and the state at the times student's ancestors were alive.

This type of assignment gets students talking with others about their schoolwork, and will also engage families in conversation about school subjects. Any time we can give assignments like these that personally involve students in the lesson, more learning will occur. Another example: when one upper elementary math unit included learning about area and square feet, for a homework project each student measured the rooms of his or her house or apartment. The students then calculated the area and perimeter of the rooms and of the whole residence. In class, they used these dimensions to build scale model houses using sugar cubes.

Here is another homework assignment:

Dear Students,

Your homework for the next week is to interview your parents and find out the following things:

1. What is your parent's job? (What do they do on their job?)

2. What MATH do your parents or parent do on their job? (add, subtract, multiply, divide, geometry, algebra, etc.) Ask them to give you a sample if they can.

3. What type of READING do they do on their job? (informational or pleasure) Do they read books, papers, computer, etc.? Ask for a sample.

5. What SPEAKING do they do at work? Do they:
a. give speeches
b. talk with customers
c. talk with other employees
d. talk on the phone
e. never talk to anyone?

Give examples if possible.

Please don't wait until the last minute to interview your parents. Ask them for examples if they can get them for you. Write this up neatly to be turned in as a quality piece of work. This will be due on Tuesday, January 31.

After doing this assignment, students might use the information they obtained for other learning activities, such as constructing graphs showing the frequency with which their parents use these skills.

One way to help bring meaning and relevance to schoolwork is to link many varied activities in ongoing projects, such as play production, student-run businesses, or community service. Students sometimes complete portions of these projects at home. We create units around themes we call Central Study, which often culminate in a performance or other public activity and involve parents and the community. For example, a Central Study of oceans involved students in learning about marine habitats, the animals and plants living in them, the aquatic food web, currents and weather, boats and sailing, and more. They constructed displays, models, dioramas, and books on these topics. They assembled the "Ocean Wing of the *Morado* Natural History Museum," and invited parents one evening to attend an opening reception for their museum.

A study of the American Civil War included reading from journals of soldiers and their families, writing historical narratives and fictional journals from a soldier's point of view, learning about slavery, cotton growing and manufacture, crafts, cooking and songs from the era, and geography. As a culminating activity, all the school's students and staff members gathered at school on a Saturday for a Civil War reenactment. Carrying backpacks, they marched to a local park, where they camped out for the day. They saw a demonstration of rifle handling, tried quilting, and saw a battle reenacted. A student remembers the day like this:

One big thing that we did was when we were all learning about the Civil War, we actually had a day of a life of a soldier. We all came to school at 5 o'clock in the morning cause that was when a soldier usually awoke. We brought all our things like bags and all the art supplies and drinks. We had a breakfast, corn muffins and tea. Then we marched all the way on a trail. I guess it was two miles and then back, so that's about four miles and then we went walking some more when we got there. We learned how to march because some guys came and taught us how to march and then acted out part of a battle. Then we had lunch, some kind of hard bread kind of like a cracker [hardtack], and then we did a lot of activities and it was really fun.

Learning Family Play

Involving students in a production is an effective way for them to learn by doing things that they see as useful and meaningful. An example is the musical play, *Take Care of Our Mother the Earth,* which the *Morado* learning family (upper elementary) is producing and planning to perform for parents. Many of the group's school days for the past several weeks have been filled with preparations and related activities. This afternoon, students are rehearsing some of the musical numbers they will perform. They practice songs that the whole company sings, and one lip-synch number. After the songs, the students take up their musical instruments for the instrumental numbers. These are not the usual band instruments; but instead, various shakers, horns, drums, and other percussion instruments which the students themselves designed and constructed. Along with music, the play has several speaking parts, jobs for stage crew, set designers and builders, and work in costume design, prompting, and all other aspects of the production, including a videotape recording of the performance.

It is interesting to watch students learning during this time; they are all focused, happy, and productive. Because they care about putting on a quality performance, students see their work as useful, and they cooperate in working toward the goal. Each child uses several modes of learning, stimulating those that might be less developed, and also choosing tasks that are appropriate to their strengths. Putting on this kind of musical play is one way we integrate visual and performing arts into the curriculum. The experience helps students to see an art form as a useful and important part of their lives.

Teachers Jan Lukow and Anne Schatz had the idea of producing a play when they wanted to plan a Central Study unit on the theme of sound for their third-, fourth- and fifth-grade students. Anne Schatz said,

167

We find that our creativity is freed by working on things we teachers have a real interest in. We see a lot more opportunities to tie in various curriculum units that we need to teach. It works better than worrying first about the specific outcomes--that can cause too much stress, and it is more difficult to make the lessons interesting enough to keep students' attention.

They have integrated several learning goals into this production. The environmental theme of *Take Care of Our Mother the Earth* links to a recently completed study of recycling. Having students present the play in public, and advocate caring for the Earth, will promote their becoming conscientious citizens. As part of the study unit on sound, students learned about acoustics as related to speaking and being heard in a room, and increased their understanding by rehearsing parts for the play. Using skills of visual-spatial thinking and manual manipulation, they created and built models of imaginary rooms, including furniture and contents, which would have sound-reflective and sound-absorbing qualities. While designing instruments, they planned and executed original designs, practiced dexterity, and increased their understanding of how sound works by learning about the scientific concepts of tones, vibration, resonance, and absorption and reflection of energy.

They also investigated structure and function of the ear. On the wall in the classroom, a bulletin board display titled "Ideal Ears" presents photographs of students, each wearing a pair of ears that he or she designed and constructed of cardboard. All are different, with several examples of large, funnel-shaped structures, reflecting what children learned about the ways sound waves are collected and concentrated by animals' outer ears.

Displays of all these projects, posters (illustrating sound terms, process writing, animal ears, the human ear, and more) and student writing and artwork are everywhere in the double classroom. This visual richness of the environment is purposeful. Research on human learning, such as explained and documented in *Brain-Based Learning & Teaching*, by Eric Jensen (1995), shows that children perceive such peripheral elements and learn from them. Seeing posted facts and descriptions of processes every day provides the repeated exposure that helps students remember what they learn. Making these objects themselves helps this process even more. Also, students, teachers, and visiting parents all enjoy the contents of the room for the colorful, lively atmosphere they help create, and the sense of accomplishment students feel when they see all the things they have done.

To add more learning experiences during the study of sound, teachers invited parents of learning family members to volunteer as visiting speakers. One, a jet engineer, brought an oscilloscope to show to the students, and taught them how sound can be represented visually by graphs of wave patterns. Students were fascinated by his explanations of how sound resonance can cause such extreme vibrations that aircraft parts can be damaged and even break, and how engineers design to keep this from happening. Another parent brought a small group of her hearing impaired students to visit and show how they use sound. *Morado* students saw the visitors' hearing aids, learned how they amplify sounds, and learned a few words and letters of American Sign Language. They learned that, as one boy said, the visitors "are hearing impaired, but they are normal kids other than hearing." He went on,

> I never knew that people with impaired hearing can talk on the phone, but they can. They have a specially designed electronic thing that goes on the telephone to make the sound louder. Sometimes they have a light that flashes so they know when the phone is ringing.

Several life skills were practiced during the unit on sound, and various types of intelligence were used.*

* "I have posited that all human beings are capable of at least seven different ways of knowing the world...According to this analysis, we are all able to know the world through language, logical-mathematical analysis, spatial representation, musical thinking, the use of the body to solve problems or to make things, an understanding of other individuals, and an understanding of ourselves. There individuals differ is in the strength of these intelligences— the so-called *profile of intelligences*—and in the ways in which such (cont.)

- Interpersonal skills of cooperation and mutual support were necessary to get everything done. Working on the play did a lot to bring the members of the learning family closer together and strengthen the family-like feeling of belonging.
- Keeping the chaos organized and everyone on task strengthened students' organizational skills, and they learned more about persisting with a project over the long term.
- Verbal expression and memorization were exercised as students rehearsed their parts, and musical and rhythmic intelligence used as they learned and performed the songs and played their instruments.
- Students got some practice in interpersonal problem solving and intrapersonal self-management. When some children were slow to learn the lines for their parts in the play, others got into arguments with them about not being responsible enough. The teachers called a family meeting to discuss working together, and reminded everyone that people learn in different styles at different rates. Students made the self-evaluation that getting angry did not help them get closer to their goals. They then tried out constructive ways to give and receive help, by role-playing possible things they might say to each other.
- Visual-spatial intelligence was used to design and decorate props and sets. Logical-mathematical skills were practiced as real-life story problems as students designed and calculated dimensions. To construct the sets and props, they exercised bodily-kinesthetic intelligence.
- Bodily-kinesthetic, musical, and linguistic intelligences were practiced as students rehearsed and performed their roles with non-verbal expression as well as words.

(*note, continued) intelligences are invoked and combined to carry out different tasks, solve diverse problems, and progress in various domains." (Gardner 1995, p. 12)

Community Service as Useful Learning: Casey's Restaurant

At the elementary school level, children enjoy being able to help others. To enable them to do this and also to meet some of their need for love and belonging, one of the things we have done is to adopt Casey's Restaurant in downtown Grand Rapids. Casey's provides low-cost meals to homeless and needy residents of our city, and each learning family is involved once each year in a project for the restaurant.

One year, students carried out a restaurant project of their own, preparing and serving meals to parents (which provided abundant learning experiences in formulating and solving problems, mathematical calculation, organization, business practices, the physical processes of preparing and serving food, and other skills). Instead of having a Christmas party for themselves with the money their restaurant earned, the children decided to use the funds to help others. They purchased turkey, cheese, fresh fruit and other supplies, baked homemade cookies, and made 400 sack lunches. Accompanied by several parents, teachers, and their principal, students went to Casey's Restaurant to serve the lunches, pour coffee, and clean the tables for the people there.

For a recent project, *Amarillo* and *Morado* learning families decided to collect hygiene products to distribute at Casey's. Students made posters and advertisements encouraging all students and their families to donate soap, shampoo, deodorant, and other toiletry items. They put large containers in the hallways at school to collect the donations.

They were surprised to find that their helping endeavor reached beyond the school and the people at Casey's; one of the secretaries at the district administration office read a copy of the Huntington Woods Parent Action Team newsletter there, and noticed the appeal from our students for donations. She thought it was a very good idea, and even told her 82-year-old mother about it. Her mother was so impressed to hear that these young people were reaching out to others in need that she gathered a few toiletry items herself. She sent them to the office with her daughter, who then sent them through the interschool mail to us. Her mother then talked to one of her elderly friends about the project, and that woman was so enthusiastic about it that *she* bought some hygiene items and sent them to Huntington Woods as her donation.

When the donated items had come in, the students made friendship cards. Then they set up an assembly line to put muffins and containers of orange juice into individual bags, and staple a friendship card to the outside of each one. Then the students, their parents, and teachers took everything downtown to Casey's, where they distributed the snacks and the hygiene products.

These projects promote useful learning in several ways. For example, when students bake cookies to put in sack lunches, they practice practical math skills of using fractions, measurements, and calculating, and the life skills of baking and cleanup. Setting up the assembly lines to make sandwiches and assemble sack lunches, they learn about hygienic food handling and efficient production. Through serving members of the community, they gain personal satisfaction and realize their connection to others. After serving lunches at Casey's, one student said, "The people really enjoyed it...We have to get used to working with and helping other people. I think everybody should do it." The appreciation of the people who receive their donations has meant a lot to the children. They were given this poem written by one of the men they served:

The Cherubs of Charity, by William James Lubben

You keep hearing that there's no such thing
    as a free lunch
that whenever you're helped your benefactor wants something in
    return
Well we had a free lunch here folks
    courtesy of those kids from Huntington Woods.
They assembled paper bags and wax paper
    around fruit, meat and bread
Bags complete with artwork and snowflakes
    and short sweet messages about friendship
We all eat some kind of meal every day
    but not always with a personal touch

They visited our tables with food and coffee
   like angels
It's good to know in the cold winter
   that some children have warm hearts
their gain was in simple giving
our gain was in being fed and cared about.

P.S. Please come back and do this again. I remember last year.
Thanks. W.J.L.

Huntington Woods also offers many other opportunities for useful learning, such as

- Adopting a neighborhood park where many of the students play after school. Students pick up litter and plant flowers there.
- Planning, preparing and cultivating gardens on the school grounds, including compost making. Along the way students learn the sciences involved, studying soil, botany, climate, solar angles and position, and weather. The flowers and vegetables grown are donated to shelters and Casey's Restaurant.
- Learning family businesses, which in our school are very active. Students create and operate businesses to make and sell products or provide services. They learn to do market research, develop business plans, plan and carry out production, keep accounts, and evaluate the results of their efforts. One year, parents were invited to a Business Exposition to see all the businesses in operation and buy the products.
- The Garageless Garage Sale of donated items from students' homes. Students priced the articles, arranged displays, and sold items to parents and students, making change and keeping records of their earnings.
- The Job Corps, in which each third-, fourth-, and fifth-grade student has a job helping to operate the school. Every day students raise the flags in the morning and put them away in the afternoon, shovel show in winter, serve lunch, collect materials for recycling, replace paper towels and toilet tissue in restrooms, or help the secretary by running copies or completing paperwork.

Students feel like valuable members of their school when they are involved in caring for the facility and receiving recognition for their work. The jobs rotate every few weeks, according to a schedule worked out by students who apply to work as Job Corps managers. In addition to helping students learn lifelong practical skills, Job Corps helps eliminate vandalism problems.

- Project Checkbook, in which students bank the 'play money,' or scrip, which they earn from jobs. They balance their checkbooks and pay bills for expenses such as taxes, utilities, rent, and insurance. Student auditors check periodically for accuracy of the records, and bill student 10 cents scrip for every mistake. (Some students plan ahead and save money by asking a friend to pre-audit their checkbook for 5 cents per error.)

Teaching Reading

The most important part of teaching reading is to convince students to put reading into their quality worlds as something they want to do. Once they are "hooked" by enjoyable reading experiences, they readily work on improving their skills. Students select anything that they would like to read, and we help them read it. We use a lot of literature for reading. Since we do not buy expensive textbooks, we can afford a large selection of trade paperback books. Each learning family collects a wide-ranging assortment of materials for students to read: magazines, comic books, fiction books, non-fiction, sports cards, and more. Students also bring things from home that they are interested in reading. We think that as long as the children are reading, that is what counts.

Recognizing that different children learn to read in different ways, teachers at our school have developed a very eclectic approach. They group students in various ways for reading lessons at different levels or of different types. Some of our students seem to learn best with a controlled vocabulary system for reading. They respond well to old basal readers (which we bought used), which they read in small groups and individually.

We do a lot of work with whole-language learning, which has "proved successful at setting a context for literacy activities while at the same time helping students to acquire the basics that will allow them eventually to read and write on their own" (Gardner 1991, page 211). This approach involves activities such as reading a big book to students and having them follow along with their smaller books, and then doing a number of activities related to the story read. Students who are independent readers are assigned sections of books to read, which they have all week to complete; then they write about what they have read. Teachers do a lot of teaching through paired reading, matching students from older learning families one-to-one with students from younger learning families. Twice a week, the pairs meet and read stories together.

Many young children learn well through phonetic instruction. For those who do, we involve them in a phonics game which uses cards. Teachers train fourth-grade students, who then each become responsible for tutoring two first-grade students through the phonics program. Fourth-grade student Colleen is one who finds that her younger partners are enthusiastic about playing:

> I go to play the phonics card game with my partners, and they are learning a lot. The game is fun so they play it as long as we have time for. When it's time for me to go back to my learning family, Bryan says, Do you *have* to stop now?' He would play it with me all day if he could! He's good at it, too.

We have individual silent reading that lasts from fifteen minutes to one hour each day. Occasionally, each learning family has a 'Read-In' for which students bring pillows and cushions from home, and everyone spends part of a day reading whatever they choose. We know the children are reading, not just staring at their books during the silent reading periods, because teachers confer with each student three or four times each week. They ask the students, "Tell me a little bit about what you are reading. What have you learned? What are the characters doing?" and students can discuss what they have read.

To keep things interesting, we change the format fairly often. For instance, instead of individual reading, teachers might switch to whole group reading for awhile, or introduce a new Reader's Theater play or other project.

We believe that the more children write, the better they will be able to read, so learning families spend time each day in journal writing, story writing and writing reports. Students are involved in writing video scripts, commercials for their businesses for television broadcast, and dialog for plays. Students are helped to write letters to grandparents or other relatives, who are often delighted to correspond with the children.

We initiate many language experience stories. When classes have been on field trips or involved in an activity, they write a group story together about it. That gives the teacher the opportunity to model good writing skills, and some teachable moments for teaching vocabulary, punctuation, sentence structure, and paragraphs. Students are then able to read the story that they all have written together. Often we word-process and print a copy of the story for each student, leaving space on the pages for each child to illustrate the story. Then students take the stories home and read them to their parents.

Our work with Readers' Theater and other productions helps give children a purpose for reading. They know that if they are performing those parts for an audience, it is important that they read fluently and with expression.

Young students learn to evaluate their reading progress by reading into a tape recorder, with the help of parent volunteers or older tutors, and listening to the tape. Every couple of months, they read onto a tape again, and then are asked to listen to both (or several) tapes to assess their progress, with the help of some rubrics we have designed. Children often share these tapes with their parents at their student-led conferences.

The things that we do as part of the normal running of the school involve students in reading; they write letters to each other in our Post Office program, and do a lot of reading in Job Corps and in the banking program. Students even found that in order to build the shed successfully (an Intersession project; see page 39), they needed to use their reading and writing skills. The directions that came with the shed kit took careful reading so that the builders would know how the parts went together, and in what order. After a crew finished a building session, they wrote a report for the next crew, so that they knew where to pick up in the directions.

In 1996, after testing all our lower elementary students in reading and comprehension, we found that most of our first and second grade students are reading above grade level. For older students who are not yet reading well, we primarily emphasize getting them to put reading into their quality worlds as something that they want to do. For some, that might mean that we build models with them and help them read the directions, so that they associate reading with the fun and accomplishment of putting together the model. After the kids have constructed a model, we help them write a story about it, which they can read. We know that children will not expend the effort necessary to learn to read well unless they see that it is useful to them and will add quality to their lives.

Reading Intervention Program

Julio speaks Spanish as his first language, and has struggled with reading. Although he is several months into the third grade, a reading comprehension assessment showed him to be functioning at a first-grade level. His learning family sets aside time for students to read silently each day, but Julio does not really enjoy it. Often he would rather talk to the children near him, but they don't like being bothered and prevented from reading their books, and the teachers are not happy with the disruption. One day Julio's teacher asks him, "Would you go with Mrs. Lichti for a short talk? She has some ideas that might help you enjoy reading more." Julio assents. He already knows who Mrs. Lichti is, and that she smiles often and is nice to kids.

On the way down the hall, Sarah Lichti and Julio chat. She asks him a few questions to bring her up to date on activities she knows the boy likes: whether he played hockey with his brothers yesterday after school (he did, and scored some goals), whether he has any new hockey cards, if his new baby sister has learned to smile

177

yet. Julio relaxes as he speaks, and becomes quite animated about these subjects.

The two sit down in a quiet room for their talk, and Sarah says, "I would like to hear a little bit about your reading. How is it going for you?" At first he says, "It's okay," but when she asks for specifics, such as "What books are you reading?" and "Would you say it is easy for you, or hard?" Julio mentions an "easy book" that he likes (she recognizes it as a pre-first-grade book), but says that the books his friends read are too hard. She shares with him the results of his reading assessment. "You are now in third grade, and your reading test showed that you are reading and understanding at about a mid-first-grade level. Is that okay for you?" Julio answers, "No, that's not so good."

"Would you like to improve so that you can read better?"

"Yes."

"Okay. Do you want me to help you figure out a plan to help your reading go better? So you could read at a third-grade level, or maybe even better?"

"Yeah, I really do. If my reading gets better, I won't feel so dorky when everybody is reading."

"Okay. Let's talk about things that work to help you learn reading. When Mrs. Blackwell played the word families game with you, did that help?"

"Yes, that helped a lot. I learned some letters and sounds, and the game was fun."

They continue, with the teacher mentioning several instructional strategies that Julio has experienced, such as phonics instruction, being read to, basal readers, books on tape, computer programs, studying word families, etc. For each one, she asks if that instructional strategy seemed to help, and Julio is very capable of telling her which ones seemed to help, and which did not help at all. With Julio's help, she develops a plan that includes nine activities for him to do every day. Some he will do alone, others with the help of various adults. She tells him, "Mrs. Mentley, Mrs. Blackwell [an instructional paraprofessional], your teachers, and I will all help you with this, and we will talk to you about it any time you want. If you find out that part of it is not helping you, we will be happy to help you figure out a new plan that will work better. Will you talk to us sometimes about how it is going?" Julio says that he will.

"We want you to follow this plan for two months," she goes on. "After that, we will give you another reading test to see how much you have improved. Is that okay with you?" and Julio consents to this. They converse for a few minutes more before parting. Sarah encourages him, and Julio seems happy and hopeful of improvement. He makes a firm verbal commitment to carry out the plan.

Six weeks later, Julio is very, very proud of the progress he has made in his Reading Intervention Plan. When Mrs. Mentley asks him one day how his reading is going, he answers, "I'm really getting a lot better. Today I was reading some first-grade and some second-grade pages, and even a third-grade book, and I was doing really, really good. My brain is working harder now I'm on this reading plan."

Huntington Woods students are performing very well overall and having great success, but there are a few students who still were not reading as well as we would like. We decided to put together Reading Intervention Plans to improve the students' reading, which would improve their confidence levels and their happiness in school.

Each teacher was asked to submit names of students he or she thought were not reading well. Then Kaye Mentley and Sarah Lichti tested each of these students to assess reading comprehension, using the Stiegflitz Informal Reading Inventory. The twelve students whose testing showed they were reading below grade level were then considered our "pool" of students for intervention. An important note here is that, because we do not identify Special Education students at Huntington Woods, this group of students included children who, at other schools, would be called educably mentally impaired and severely learning disabled.

It is crucial that, before we start any programs with a student's instruction, we help the student understand the goal, agree to the goal, and then become a part of the plan for improving learning in the subject area. When we talked with the students about the results of the reading comprehension assessment, we were not at all surprised to find that all of the children want to read well.

By involving students in the plan right away, and asking what kind of things seemed to help their reading, we learned a lot from them about their different learning styles and which strategies worked for them. Then, with each student's help, we designed a plan that he or she would follow, most including from eight to ten strategies that the student would do daily. With some of the students, strategies included parent involvement, such as doing paired reading at home. We held training sessions at school to show parents how to do this activity. We only involved the parents, though, where we were confident that they would follow through consistently with their children.

One of the strategies used with all the students is called "Write to Read." With this strategy, the student would sit next to an adult at a keyboard and dictate a story, or anything he or she wanted to have written down, and the adult would word-process what the student said and make the necessary edits and corrections. This then became a part of the student's reading for the day. Our experience bears out Dr. Glasser's observations that writing is a wonderful way to help students learn to read well.

Adam, a student who worked in the Reading Intervention program, had the idea to write "101 Quality Things about Huntington Woods." Here are some of the things he thought of:

I love the teachers at HW and I know that they love me, too!
I get to eat with my teachers in my own room instead of in a noisy cafeteria.
I like the work that they give us because it's fun work instead of boring work.
I like to work out problems by talking about it instead of going to detention without even talking.
I like having class meetings to talk about problems or talk about what is going on during the day. I always know what to be prepared for.
We sit at tables with our friends instead of at desks.
I love how the teachers do experiments or show examples so we can see it before we try it.

My teachers showed a hurricane machine. It makes a
hurricane out of steam.
We have silent reading for 20 minutes at the end of each day.
This helps us read better because we get time to practice.
I get to be on an Action Team because I'm in upper el
[elementary]. I am on the Hospitality team.
We have newspaper clippings posted all through the halls.
They tell about the First Quality School in the Nation,
Huntington Woods, the Cool School. I have never seen so
many newspaper clippings at any school.
I get help in different subjects from four different teachers
besides my own.
We have a picnic outside in the summer. I get to help serve
lunch.
We have work breaks at different times so it's not so
crowded. Our teachers take us outside after we have
worked a lot and we need a break.
I used the reading program and my reading comprehension
went up three grades.

When Adam had finished his   "101 Quality Things about
Huntington Woods," he started writing books. He wrote and
published two chapter books, one an imaginative mystery story with a
young boy called Adam as the main character. Sarah Lichti said:

When he started the 101 Quality Things, finishing 25
things in one day, and then the next day adding many more,
Adam really felt proud of himself. The last two days we
worked on it took much longer because it was harder to get
new ideas, and he felt even more pride when he finished.
When we were checking the spelling on it, he was so excited
that he kept saying, 'Okay, now print! Now print!' He couldn't
wait to get the final product in his hand. When he did, he said,
'I'd better take it right down to Mrs. Mentley to show her,'
because he knew what a quality piece of writing it was, and
that everyone would be proud of him for it. He gets a lot of
praise for it from other students and all the teachers.
When Adam was working on his first chapter book, he
was always so excited to come in and work with me on it. He
would say, 'My Mom can't wait to hear the next chapter, so I

just have to finish my new chapter today." His aunts and cousin were all waiting to read it once he finished. I saw so much pride in Adam over that story. He wanted to show it to Kaye, and to his teachers and family. It was remarkable to see.

When asked about his achievements, Adam said,

I feel very proud of myself, that I know so much about my school and about how it is quality. When I see it [my project], I feel like I'm special. A lot of kids say, 'hey, did you do all those?' and I tell them, 'Yeah.' The teachers and Mrs. Mentley are proud of me, and my Mom too. I printed it out and brought it home to show my mom. I did my chapter book, too, a mystery story of six chapters, all eight or nine pages long. I feel good about myself when I look at that. I think I have a really good imagination if I can come up with that much stuff. I'm happy about how my grades went up and my reading is better.

In two months, Adam gained three years grade equivalence in reading comprehension. He also passed the mandatory state test in reading.

Reading their own stories helps overcome some of the traditional difficulties in helping older students who are not reading well; very often the books at the students' reading achievement level are written for younger children, and the students do not want to read them. Composing their own stories enables students to read things that they have written and are interested in.

We also learned from one student that he did not want to read books at his level in class, because he felt embarrassed. We talked to him about the idea of a book cover, and he became excited about that possibility. So, for several students, we made up book covers that they could put onto their books, and then no one knew what they were reading. In order to add to the "camouflage" we also made some book covers for other kids, and distributed them at random, so that many of our students now have book covers.

During the process of developing the students' plans and their committing to following them, we explained to each student that we would like him or her to follow this plan for two months, and then we would give another test to see if we were making improvement. We were careful to let the student know that if we were not seeing improvement, then we would re-work the plan at any time to come up with other strategies the student could use. As each student participated in his or her plan, we would talk with him or her frequently and ask how it was going. The kids were excited about many of the strategies they were doing, and we adults were always very eager to read what they had written or hear them read it to us.

We also approached our parent group about our desire to improve student reading. They agreed to purchase a computer and some special software in reading strategies for use by students who were involved in Reading Intervention. These arrived just two weeks before the end of the two-month program, but the students really liked the computer program, and it seemed to help them. The software is called *The Sentence Master*, originally written for mentally impaired people, and uses the concept of over learning. Total cost of the computer and software was $3000. It was wonderful to see once again how, when we are honest with our parent group about what we want to do and why, they are very eager to help. It is extremely important that all of us in the school work together to help our students do well.

With a couple of students, we rewrote plans part way through the two-month program, because the students were not enjoying the activities or were refusing to do them. At the end of two months, the students were reassessed, with these results: Julio now read with comprehension at a high third-grade level; seven others of the twelve gained from two to four grade levels; two improved one to one and a half grade levels, and two students stayed the same in reading comprehension.

For the eight students who made huge gains, we developed maintenance plans for them to follow for the next two months. These consist of fewer strategies for them to do each day, with less adult intervention. After the maintenance period, these kids then had another assessment to make sure they are maintaining their progress.

(Reassessment showed that Julio is maintaining his skills at grade level, Adam above grade level.) With the two who, for various reasons, did not make sufficient progress, we will rewrite plans with them to look for other strategies that will be more successful. We will probably make more use of the computer and reading program, and are getting a second computer for this purpose. Our goal is to have every student reading at or above grade level when entering an upper elementary learning family at the beginning of the third grade.

Using Technology Instead of Textbooks

In this, the information age, "textbooks grow obsolete quickly and do not provide real life experience for the students" (Schatz and Pifer [1996] page 23). Often schools find that they can not use large parts of textbooks because the books do not fit the state- and county-mandated outcomes they need to teach. We work with our local school board trustees, who have been very cooperative, to demonstrate that children are learning what we are charged with teaching them. As long as we can reach this goal, the board gives us freedom to choose how to accomplish it. The State of Michigan does not mandate textbooks, so we use only one, *Chicago Math*. Rather than using more textbooks, our teachers develop our own lessons and units of study, so instruction is focused directly on what we want the students to learn.

We use technology as much as possible to enhance learning. We have a twenty-seven-station computer lab, which is available to students for one-half hour at a time and also at choice time, and mini-labs in each classroom. All are on a distributed network, and can access the same software. Without the expense of textbooks, we are able to use some of the money allocated to them toward computer software. Many of our computers were provided through a district bond issue, and we wrote grants to obtain funding for some of our other technology. We also have more funds available, since we do not buy textbooks, to purchase other instructional materials and to hire people to help us teach and run the school.

In computer instruction, our students begin exposure at the kindergarten level. Keyboarding skills are taught in grade three and up. We find that the children like writing on the computers. Every student who graduates will be able to use a computer for writing and other word processing. There are many good software programs available to help students learn reading, math, writing, science, and problem solving skills. Some programs we currently have are:

- Microsoft Works for Windows. This includes some tools, programming, word processing, database and spreadsheet.
- Minesweeper and Solitaire games to develop skill in handling the mouse.
- Kids Stuff, which lets young students practice spelling simple words, learn the alphabet, count objects and find the correct numeral. It also has some beginning phonetics instruction.
- Talking Phonics Plus. For lower elementary students, this program includes consonant and vowel activities, with beginning, end and middle consonant sounds and long and short vowel sounds.
- Young Math, with beginning math skills including counting, simple addition and subtraction, recognizing larger and smaller numbers, and identifying patterns.
- Believe in Magic Library, for middle to older elementary students, includes interactive adventure stories in which students can put in events they want to have happen. Each time a student uses the program, a different story is created.
- PC USA for United States geography, and PC GLOBE for countries of the world. These have maps of the states and countries, with information about each one, including the state song or national anthem. They are used like an electronic encyclopedia.
- Math Blaster Plus. This program provides timed drills in the basic math processes of addition, subtraction, multiplication and division, and helps students increase their speed in using them. The level of difficulty can be adjusted, so it works for students of all ages.

185

- Sprout, for planning a vegetable garden. Students input our climatic region, use the computer generated timeline for gardening activities and the generated lists for shopping requirements, and so on.
- Carmen San Diego, a geography adventure game in which students follow clues, using atlases and other sources and tools, to find Carmen's whereabouts.
- Mobius (KidsWare), for young students. It includes programs for planning a neighborhood, creating an animal, music, counting, word processing, beginning reading, nursery rhymes, art, and a paint program that involves mixing colors and creating designs. It can be done in English or in Spanish, and gives directions audibly so that even children just starting to read can use it.

As soon as students become able to read independently, they participate in our Integrated Learning System program, which functions as an "electronic textbook" to teach skills in math, reading and problem solving. Unlike a printed textbook, the ILS opens to a separate page for each student, depending on the results of the student's last test! It gives students assessments and then appropriate instruction in basic reading, math, and writing skills. Each student progresses at his or her own pace. The ILS has a monitoring system that allows teachers to see where each student is working at any given time, select lessons as necessary, and decide where they might want to provide some more opportunities for learning.

We also use computers for students who have difficulty with fine motor skills. For example, one of our first-grade students has a neurological disorder that makes it difficult for him to write. He does all of his spelling tests and writing assignments on the computer instead of writing by hand. As students learn to do quality work, they also learn that the best place to do it is on the computer, which makes it much easier for them to edit their work and make improvements. The computer programs that we have also help us with music production (students are able to learn how to compose and read music and play a keyboard) and with science instruction and art.

Having classrooms each equipped with a TV, VCR, telephone and computer mini-lab allows us to teach students in a learning environment that is much more like what they will encounter in their future workplaces and homes. We have a steerable satellite dish that enables us to receive broadcasts from around the world. Some of the students' favorites are those that come from Sea World.

Parent-teacher communication is facilitated by having the telephones in classrooms. Schools often ask teachers to have more frequent communication with parents, but in many schools there are only two or three telephones available. We find that having a phone for each teacher helps them develop good communication more easily. Students are also able to use the telephones to access information for reports, call their parents, and so on. For example, when students undertook to compute costs for a trip around Michigan, they used the telephones to find information on motel rates, vehicle mileage, and gasoline prices.

Students learn from using our video recording and editing equipment, and enjoy it a great deal. With our in-house video system, we are able to do school-wide broadcasts of shows that students produce. We have had students make commercials for many of our school businesses and broadcast them on this system, and some students have also done news shows. Any time students are doing a special activity in their classroom such as a play or a musical, they broadcast it for other classes to watch if they would like to.

Our experience with Daniel exemplifies how we used technology with one student to get him to put school into his quality world as a place he wants to be. Daniel came to Huntington Woods as an older student with a chip on his shoulder against school. Throughout most of the year he was not very cooperative, and he certainly was not doing high quality work. Part way through the school year, when we decided to make a short videotape about HW, we approached Daniel to see if he would be interested in helping with the camera work and editing. That really seemed to get him excited, and each day he began to enjoy school more. He became very involved, and soon was even volunteering to stay after school to clean and put things in order, so that the rooms would look better as background in his camera shots. He and another student worked with a cameraman from a local public access television station, and together they developed a twelve-minute video about our school. Since then, Daniel seems to enjoy school so much more. and his school work has improved.

When a reporter interviewed him and asked about how he liked school, Daniel spoke about how much he likes it, said he doesn't mind going to school in the summertime, and even said how much has always liked Huntington Woods. After the interview, Kaye asked him why he had not been completely truthful with the reporter. Daniel's response was, "I'm really starting to like this school, and I don't want to say anything that might hurt its reputation!"

Daniel is now at the middle school, where he has become a real leader of his class; he is a Student Council officer, and his grades on his report card are all "A's." His mother is very pleased with his progress, and he is, too.

Learning Choice Theory

Efforts to transform a school will fail unless the principal and the staff fully understand and internalize the psychological framework for quality. The staff must then have the opportunity to develop the skills that will allow them to align their actions with the theory...They must establish a staff development program to build a common foundation of knowledge for all staff members...[which] must embody the same principles and practices as the quality program for students learners.

--Crawford, et.al. (1994, pages25, 42)

Teaching, administrative and support staff members are committed to using Choice Theory, Reality Therapy and lead management throughout Huntington Woods School. Staff training in the concepts and their application is ongoing, with any new staff members having the opportunity to start their training before employment begins or within their first year. The first step is to read William Glasser's *The Quality School*. The staff and principal have studied the book together, going over it chapter by chapter and talking through questions about each chapter, such as 'what does this mean to us?' and 'if we believe this, what might we want to change in our lives and in our school?'

The Family Council sponsors teaching staff members for the sequence of training sessions taught by the William Glasser Institute. This is an eighteen-month program taught by qualified Institute instructors to small groups. It includes sessions of intensive study of the concepts, and periods of guided practice using readings, role plays and discussion. This leads to Certification Week, during which participants demonstrate their understanding of Choice Theory and Reality Therapy concepts and their skills at using them. After certification, each participant can choose to continue training to become an instructor.

Staff members also work within the school to make sure that their skills are refreshed, refined and practiced throughout the year, using staff meetings to discuss Quality Schools and lead management, practice with role-plays, and continually evaluate their progress. Many of them say that their learning extends beyond their professional lives to influence patterns of thinking and interacting with their families, friends and acquaintances. Teaching Assistant Peggy Lubke told of one example which occurred early in her training, while she was in the Basic Intensive Week:

> We were studying the idea of the quality world, and one of the things I identified as being in my quality world is a great relationship with my sons. Then I started to look at my behavior and realized it was sometimes working against that good relationship I want. Some days while I am at work, my boys neglect their household chores. When I get home, I often find myself getting angry and yelling at the boys--yelling at them while *I* do the unfinished chores.
>
> After the first class session, I came home in the evening and saw that my son had not unloaded the dishwasher, and I felt a flash of anger. Then just as quickly came the thought, 'If I get mad, how will that get me what I really want?' Instead of yelling, I said, 'Would you please unload the dishwasher? Any time you want to do it is fine with me.' My son said, 'I'll do it

right after this [TV] program. Okay?' So I said, 'Okay. How was your day today? Tell me a little about what you did.' He just looked at me, then he said, 'Aren't you going to yell at me?' 'No, I guess not,' I answered. Later that evening, he came and gave me a hug, and said, 'Thanks for not getting angry at us, Mom.' He seemed so happy, and I felt very close to him.

I knew that if I had yelled at him, my son probably would have cleaned up the kitchen, which I wanted. But I also want a good relationship, and for him to do his part of the household work willingly. Yelling would not help me get that, so I tried something else. Now, I have to laugh, because the boys want me to go back to yelling. They say the chores were easier when I did!

• Instructional paraprofessional Lisa Blackwell, since learning Choice Theory, has changed her interactions with students to find ways they can meet their basic needs. For example, to give them a bit more freedom, she said,

Instead of having a book ready for a particular child to read, now I lay four or five books out on the table, and ask the student, 'what would you like to read today?' They let me know, and we sit down and read it. They seem more willing to participate when they have a choice in the matter.

• Upper elementary teacher Jan Lukow finds that her new understanding of motivation reduces the stress she feels at school.

In the past, I would take on more ownership of students' behavior and worry about it, even blaming myself for it. Now I realize that I can not control the students, and it is a relief. They control themselves. I can try to help them learn a better way, and I have a lot of influence with them, but I can not be responsible for everything they do. I can lead them to a better behavior, but the choice is always theirs. It also relieves a burden knowing that teachers and the principal here understand motivation, and I will not be blamed for choices my students make.

Understanding my own behavior in the framework of Choice Theory is empowering, because I realize that I do have control over my behavior. The old idea seems to be that you never really have a mind of your own, that what you do is a response to somebody else. Instead, you really have your own choices to make.

- **Introducing Choice Theory to parents**

Parents of our students are introduced to the concepts that guide the school through ongoing workshops. They learn how we use Choice Theory, Reality Therapy, and lead management, and also how they can apply the ideas at home. The best way to introduce parents to the ideas is, first of all, to model them. For example, at a meeting for parents new to Huntington Woods, the principal will start the meeting with a 'get to know you' activity, Musical Circles, in which she asks:

- What is one thing you really like about your child?
- What do you hope your child's teacher does?
- Why did you choose Huntington Woods?

The participants are asked to move around the gym informally to music until the music stops, and then arrange themselves into small groups to discuss one of these questions. After continuing that for a few rounds and a few questions, parents are then asked to take their seats and the "official" part of the meeting begins. It consists of responses to questions that parents have written earlier. The principal and teachers discuss those questions and provide informational handouts relevant to the topics raised. Lastly, Kaye Mentley asks parents what other questions they have, and responds to those. To sum up, she then talks about the three conditions for quality and how they were built into this meeting, as they are built into school experiences for students.

The first condition for quality is a warm, supportive environment free of any coercion. This environmental tone was developed by the first activities the parents did, which let them get acquainted, laugh a little and share thoughts about their children's education. A second condition for quality is useful learning. Parents want responses to questions they have submitted, so staff members know that the answers will be perceived as useful information. The third condition for quality is self-evaluation. To introduce this, Kaye concludes the presentation by asking parents to self-evaluate the information they know, think about what else they want to know, and then ask questions so that they can learn it. She points out how the conditions for quality have been integrated into the evening's meeting, and then talk about how we build the conditions into school days. In the kind of environment that meets these conditions, people will do their highest quality work.

Besides these parent meetings, the school offers ongoing workshops for parents in which they can learn more the, how the school staff uses them in design and daily operations, and how parents and their children can apply the ideas at home.

- **Teaching Choice Theory to students**

Choice Theory concepts are taught in many ways, and often incorporated into classroom activities. In the youngest grades, children are taught about the basic needs, and learn to identify varieties of behavior in themselves and classmates. They talk with their teachers about what they want when they behave in particular ways. Teachers use class meetings to teach about responsibility for behavioral choices, and the problem-solving approach of Reality Therapy.

Lower elementary teachers use visual aids such as a stuffed toy bear named Happy Bear, and a chair with each leg labeled as a basic need to illustrate the importance of meeting these needs in a balanced way. A model car and its parts serve an analogy total behavior. Older children use their literature response journals to identify expressions of basic needs and quality world pictures by the characters they read about.

Role plays are employed with students of all ages. They are fun for the participants and the audiences, and in a memorable way. One day, to show four- and five-year-old students how people control their own choices, teacher Sarah Lichti and instructional paraprofessional

Kathy VanEssen play two students who are having a problem. One wants to draw when the rest of the class is drawing, but the child next to her is bothering her, tickling her and drawing on her paper. The adults act out alternative behaviors available in such a situation. First, Kathy (playing the child who is being bothered) whines "Stop that!" and, when Sarah continues trying to scribble on her paper, threatens, "I'm going to tell!" and makes a face as if she is about to cry. Sarah replies, "You'd better not," and the two argue for a minute. Then the adults step out of character, and ask the class to think about how well Kathy's behavior worked to get Sarah to leave her alone. The children are unanimous in saying that it did not work at all.

Sarah and Kathy then act another version of such a situation; when Sarah scribbles and tickles, Kathy laughs and squirms away, then tickles Sarah until both "girls" are laughing and noisy. They stop again and discuss this scene with the class. Did Kathy get Sarah to stop bothering her? "No," the children say. Did their tickling and laughing interfere with the learning of others in the room? "Yes." Was this responsible? "No, it was not."

The adults then show another possible choice for Kathy; this time, she asks Sarah politely, "Please stop doing that." When Sarah bothers her again, she gets up and goes to sit in another chair. This, the class agrees, is a better way to handle the situation. A last scene demonstrates Kathy asking the teacher to tell Sarah to stop drawing on her paper, and this, too, works successfully.

"These young children understand the concepts of Choice Theory," Sarah Lichti said. "They learn very enthusiastically and when a situation arises, they remember that they can decide what to do to get what they want in a responsible way."

Teachers at Huntington create their own materials to teach these ideas. For example, Marilyn Spreng has developed a series of lessons for lower elementary students, based on Dr. Seuss stories, which incorporate Choice Theory and also include math, language arts, and science exercises.

One of her lessons teaches about the need for freedom, using *Horton Hatches an Egg*:

Horton Hatches an Egg

Before reading, tell about how Dr. Seuss got the idea for this book. He was drawing a picture of an elephant and the picture flew out the window and landed on a tree branch.

Questions:
* What does 100% mean? Relate to doing our best, and Quality.
* Who had freedom? (Mayzie)
* Did Mayzie get in the way of someone else meeting his need for freedom? (Yes)
* Did Horton have to sit on the egg? Did he have a choice?

Activities:
* Draw pictures or write about times you are given a choice (Work Sheet on choices is a grid with spaces for 'working at school,' 'playing at school,' 'working at home,' 'playing at home,' and 'choices made alone,' 'choices made with friends,' and 'choices made with family.'
* Make picture and bar graphs responding to: Should Mayzie or Horton get to keep the bird elephant?
* Write about Horton and the bird elephant's first day at home in the jungle.
* Think of a favorite animal. Draw a picture of a bird with some characteristics of your animal. Review bird characteristics (lays brittle eggs, has feathers, is warm blooded, and breathes with lungs).
* (Work Sheet) List all the activities you think Mayzie did for one week while in Palm Beach. Work with a partner or alone.

Journal: I get to make choices about...

Teachers also use workbooks, Readers' Theater, and poster and collage-making activities to teach choice theory. Students in the upper elementary *Verde* learning family made "quality world T-shirts" in their study of basic needs and the quality world. Each child cut out a T-shirt shape from a large sheet of paper, then drew pictures on it to represent his or her own quality world pictures. The teacher has drawn a quality world T-shirt, too, and all of these are posted as a colorful display, with the title "Our Quality Worlds," on the classroom window.

One T-shirt is decorated with drawings of a bicycle, a person watching television, someone reading a book, and friends playing together on one sleeve, the area that stands for fun. On the other sleeve are things that meet the need for freedom, such as a picture of a convenience store where the student likes to go, and a child riding a horse. At the bottom, representing power, he has drawn himself leading a group of children. This child's quality world picture for belonging is in the center, and shows a smiling child outside a house, with two dogs nearby.

Kaye Mentley also teaches Choice Theory to fifth-grade students. In her lesson about quality world pictures, students write and draw their perceptions of things and people that are most need-fulfilling for them. To guide them, Kaye tells the students,

> Write down something you are passionate about--that you really, really care about and that is exciting, or that you are willing to go to a lot of effort to experience. Is your passion related to school, or to your personal life? Is it internal--something in yourself--or something about a relationship with someone else? What needs does it satisfy for you, or would it satisfy if you had it? Also, think about this: if you were not here, what would you most want to be doing? What do you see yourself doing two years from now? What kind of person do you want to become?

The students think seriously during this exercise about things they value. One student writes "To be a good leader for others" in his quality world; another, "A good relationship with my parents." Kaye said later, "The students really understand these concepts, and they see their learning as a way to monitor their decisions and make good choices." Other teachers concur. Jan Lukow observed:

> I hear children use the language of Choice Theory. One might say something like, 'He made me do that,' or 'She

made me so mad,' but then another student will say, 'Well, that was your choice.' We help them put the ideas into real-life use, beyond just hearing us talk about them or seeing us model for them.

If students know that learning is enjoyable and rewarding, and that through it they can meet their needs and improve their lives, they will be ready to keep on learning as adults. That ability will prove extremely useful to them as career paths and job availability change due to technological and economic changes in our world. These young people will be far better prepared to change their knowledge and skill bases than they would be if they left school with memories of learning as an experience they would prefer to avoid.

Chapter 9

PARENTAL INVOLVEMENT

Chapter 8

PARENTAL INVOLVEMENT

We find that if we ask Huntington Woods parents for what we need to improve students' learning, we get it. There is not a single thing our children's parents won't do for us. Our school has 150 to 200 hours per week of volunteer time that is donated by parents, which is just a wonderful asset for us. Obviously, it helps us do a lot of things we would not be able to do without that kind of help-- that is the equivalent of six full-time teacher aides! So we are very thankful.

--Kaye Mentley

How does a school of 370 students get parents so enthusiastic that they donate 150 to 200 hours of volunteer time to the school *each week*? How do we induce 220 parents to sign up for volunteer work on Parent Action Teams?

Beatrice Darling, mother of three Huntington Woods students, is helping out in the secretary's office today. At the desk, she appears to be cheerfully handling two or three tasks at once, supervising a student who is sorting notices for teachers' mailboxes, writing out a list of teachers and staff members in response to a request (she knows all of them, from speech therapist to night custodian), and answering the telephone. When two young boys walk into the office, she greets them familiarly, and gives her full attention to their questions. As the boys leave, satisfied, she answers a phone call from a parent who is inquiring about enrollment. He is a young father considering Huntington Woods School for his child, and is asking for information.

Mrs. Darling talks with him for several minutes and, when he asks additional questions, takes a moment to ask the principal to listen for calls, then picks up the telephone again. She talks with the caller for another fifteen minutes, saying at one point, "This school is wonderful; it is just an awesome place." She tells him that the teachers and staff are friendly, and that they make sure all students receive individual attention from their first day at school. She speaks of the progress her children have made in math and reading, how much they love their teachers, and how pleased she and her husband are with the education their children are getting. She talks about some of the things the teachers do to help children succeed in their schoolwork.

She mentions the way teachers ask students and their parents what the children are interested in learning about, and how they teach through hands-on activities. She tells a little about the classroom learning teams and how she believes they promote student involvement and social acceptance, and about tutoring by classroom peers and instructional paraprofessionals. The caller, apparently intrigued and encouraged since he keeps asking more, ends the conversation by scheduling an appointment to bring his daughter to see the school and meet Mrs. Mentley. "Your little girl Kimmy sounds like a great child," Mrs. Darling says. "Next Monday when you come in, I will be supervising a choice time activity in the gym. Please stop in and see me—I would love to meet you and your daughter."

• A local woman phones to ask if Huntington Woods would like her help as a volunteer. Even though she has no children at the school, she is looking for a volunteer job to enrich her own life. She has called six other schools to offer her time, she says, but not one of them has called her back. Kaye Mentley tells her on the telephone, "We would love to have your help. Please come in and talk to me this afternoon — we are dusting off the red carpet right now!"

- The mother of a former Huntington Woods student still volunteers to work during choice time, even though her son has gone on to middle school, because she enjoys her time with the children. She has even made a poster to promote the choice time activity she will be leading—it shows a colorful butterfly craft project.

Huntington Woods is a school of choice, which means that students enroll here because their parents choose this school. As we are a public school, we do not select students; we take them all, and keep them all. There are some myths about what it is like to be a school of choice. It is sometimes thought that since all of our parents chose this school for their children, then we must have a wonderful level of parent involvement. However, we have a significant population who are here not because they and their parents agree with our educational philosophy, but because of the extended calendar alone. That extra six weeks of free childcare, with transportation provided, is a tremendous incentive for many parents.

Also, consider who is likely to transfer their child to a new school. Is it likely to be parents of the child who loves her school, who is doing well academically and behaviorally, whose parents are involved in volunteering? Probably, more likely to move will be the ones who are dissatisfied, the parents of children who are not doing well either academically or behaviorally, and who want another school to solve these problems. So quality parent involvement does not come along with being a school of choice. We must create that involvement. We do many things specifically to get and keep the wonderful, loving parental involvement that we have.

Since we do not have a guaranteed population in any school year, we must make sure our parents and students are satisfied with the service we are providing. Everyone at this school recognizes that committed parents are crucial to our success. As Howard Gardner writes (1991, page 255),

An essential partner in any kind of educational regimen is the community...In the United States today, probably the most important agents of change in the community are the parents, in their dual roles as advocates for their children and citizens of the society...If the community fails to support the desires and standards of school people, the educators are destined to fail.

We do several things to promote parental commitment and involvement. Most important, and underlying all our efforts, is our attitude of service. Teachers and staff members keep the vision of their mission to serve the needs of our customers, who are students and their parents. Parents want to help at the school where the adults take an individual interest in their child, invite parents to raise any concerns or questions, and ask them to participate in developing the child's education. We believe it, and it works.

One example of the way we send the message that we are here to serve students and parents is our decision as a staff to park furthest from the front door, and leave the front parking area free for parents and visitors. This way they do not have to park away off in the back of the lot, and hike past the employees' cars to get to the entrance. Doing this is a simple way to send a strong message to parents, and to us, about who is important.

We are all on a first-name basis with all our students' parents. Because we want to collaborate with parents in educating their children, we do not try to appear professional by distancing ourselves, but would rather become well acquainted. We give consistent attention to effective communication with parents. To involve new parents from the start, in June as soon as our lottery is completed and parents know their children are enrolled, we send them a letter. In plain language, rather than educators' jargon, the letter welcomes them to the school and invites them to a parents' meeting. At that meeting, we have some get-acquainted activities, and tell them about our philosophy. We answer their questions, and invite their input.

The following week, parents can bring their children to school for hearing and vision screening. Then they are invited to a school-wide picnic, called "Camp Explorer" (named for Huntington Woods Explorers), with games and activities for families to do together. Everyone wears a nametag. Our current parents know that if they see someone wearing a gold-trimmed nametag, he or she is a new parent, and they make a special effort to welcome the new parents, show them around, and make sure they are comfortable.

In July, we have a visitation day. Parents bring their child while school is in session, so they can see what it is like. They do some typical activities with the other students. The following week, we send them a letter regarding staffing for the next year. We offer them an opportunity to request a specific learning family for their child if they would like to. In early August, they receive a welcoming letter from their child's teachers, and also a personally written post card from the principal.

A few days before school starts in August, parents get a telephone call from one of the teachers in their child's learning family to welcome them and say, "I am looking forward to seeing you." The day before school starts, we have our open house. Parents and children can ride the buses, tour through the classrooms, and meet other parents and students.

About three weeks into the new school year, we have an all-school Expo event with a free family supper and child care provided. Students display the products of their first units of study and explain them to the parents. One week later is our Family Council kickoff meeting. We have a consultant there to do some training on how to run meetings effectively and be an effective team member. Also during the first three or four weeks, we invite parents to a curriculum night given by the teachers. They tell about what they will be teaching, what their goals are, and how they will report to parents. The first upper elementary conferences are also held in these first few weeks, for parents, students, and teachers to set goals together.

We organize several other family events, meals, and expositions each school year. Throughout the year, we solicit input with phone calls and notes, question-and-answer sessions, learning family newsletters, and student plan books which parents review each week. Our parents have the home phone numbers of the principal and teachers, and they feel free to call us at home. This way, if they work during the day, parents can easily speak to us when they are available.

We maintain an open-classroom policy in which parents are invited into classrooms all the time, and can go into any classroom without calling ahead. They are welcome to visit and observe, eat lunch with the learning family, or help out if they wish. If a parent does want to be put to work when visiting in the classroom, he or she knows where to find a task list that each learning family keeps posted. He or she can choose anything on the list that appeals, from reading with students to performing assessments and checking them, to working in the publishing center, or putting displays on the bulletin boards. Some activities can be done at home and some at school, some involve children and some do not, so parents can pick what they are most interested in and feel able to do.

Veronica Darwin said this about the open-classroom policy:

I think it's important—not just important, imperative—that people be involved in their own children's education. Education should not be left only to the teachers. I like to be in my kids' school because I like to know what's going on, and keep informed, in case when they come home from school and I ask them the traditional question 'What did you do in school today?' and they say, 'I don't remember.' So I make sure I know what they're doing in school, what they are supposed to be learning, and what they might be having trouble with, instead of just sending them off each day.

Rather than the teachers being bothered by parents' dropping by, in fact, they encourage parents to come in. So sometimes my husband, if he's around at lunchtime, will just stop in and eat lunch with my son. They invite that. They say, 'Come on in and eat lunch with your children. Come drop in anytime.' They aren't afraid to have parents in school.

Where I last taught school, many of the staff didn't really want a lot of the parents in school all the time, which was a shame. Parents were welcome to come in and help, yes, but not just to drop in unannounced. I don't know what they were afraid of. The teachers here love having people in their rooms; they appreciate having the help, and it frees them up to pay more attention to the students.

Family Council

Another thing we have done to encourage parent involvement is to change the Parent-Teacher Organization structure to a Family

Council. Parents are not required to sit through business meetings, and instead can join an action team that has a mission that matches the parent's interests. The action teams work for the school in all areas of education, from fund-raising to physical fitness.

In an article about the parents' organization at Huntington Woods, Jill Wilterdink wrote that she had noticed, in past involvement with parent-teacher organizations, that decision-making was often difficult and protracted. Also, she wrote,

> I...noticed that quite often the same people did the majority of the work...At the beginning of the school year [at Huntington Woods], parents were given the opportunity to join an Action Team that suited their interests...a choice among ten different teams that range from Public Relations to Hospitality to Parent Enrichment. This not only gives people a chance to contribute in an area of interest or expertise, but it also has proven to expedite decisions and actions. Teams have complete autonomy; they are given the "power" to manage their teams in the manner that works best for their group, and are able to make financial decisions up to a specified amount...There [is] no longer a struggle for volunteers to help with fundraisers, to host events, to run workshops; everyone knows their responsibilities. We see teams working together to provide assistance in all areas of education.
>
> Meetings are scheduled for the third Monday of each month at the school, and include childcare. This gives people a chance to interact with other team members, and helps to keep a high interest level...[the Family Council Board] meets once a month to review actions of each group and discuss financial decisions. The Board is made up of one representative from each Action Team, as well as the school principal, and is open to everyone...Having spent time in individual teams prior to this meeting, [we find that] decisions are fast and effective.
>
> ...It's incredible what gets done in these teams! In the first year, Huntington Woods Action Teams were responsible for a school brochure, Fall Festival, a monthly Parent Enrichment newsletter, seminars, welcoming new students

and much, much more. This stimulating atmosphere for parents has helped to bring the school to an average of 150 hours per week of volunteer time [*authors' note: now 200 hours on average*]...My conclusion is that the concept works...and the results speak for themselves!

Action Team members participate in a session at the beginning of the school year which teaches group working and decision-making skills. Each team sets a goal for the year, and has the autonomy to work toward achieving it and to create new goals. Each team develops strategies for meeting goals it has chosen. Action Teams strive to involve students and the community, and promote cooperation. Chairpeople of the Action Teams compose the governing body of the Family Council. They hold business meetings, open to all, where budget decisions are made. The goal, however, rather than high parent attendance at business meetings, is for large numbers of parents to participate in parent development opportunities, and to serve actively on Action Teams. (See the following page for a typical listing of Parent Action Teams.)

Family council members, like Huntington Woods' teachers, students and staff, continually evaluate the family council and re-design it as needed. Action teams and their structures can change. Goals for action teams evolve as we learn more about how to create a school where all students learn in an environment they love.

1. Physical Fitness and Nutrition Action Team
Mission - To design and implement regular physical fitness opportunities for students, staff and families.

2. Connection / Extra-Curricular Action Team
Mission - To promote unity among Huntington Woods staff, students and families and help plan and implement after-school enrichment/recreational opportunities for students.

3. Horticultural Action Team
Mission - To help plan and implement gardening and landscaping.

4. Multi-Cultural Action Team / Fine Arts Action Team
Mission - To celebrate who we are as a Huntington Woods family, using the arts.

5. Volunteer Action Team
Mission - To organize and implement a program of volunteers to help make Huntington Woods a need fulfilling school for students and adults.

6. Public Relations Action Team
Mission - To promote positive public relations for HW school.

7. Hospitality Action Team
Mission - To help students, visitors and staff see Huntington Woods as a school that is welcoming and caring for all visitors and guests.

8. Community Resources Action Team
Mission - To access resources to supplement operating funds through fund raising.

9. Technology and Curriculum Action Team
Mission - To provide parental input on curriculum and help technology be used to promote learning.

One more example of dedicated parental involvement follows: Wayne Baker, parent of a kindergarten student, has a full-time job. When the new playground equipment for Huntington Woods was delivered, he came to school to help assemble it on Friday afternoon. He was here that afternoon, Friday evening, Saturday morning and part of Saturday afternoon, working on the equipment. Because he and so many other parents came to help assemble the new equipment, the job was done in record time. The manufacturer's representative had specified that it would take about three days to complete. He was amazed when so many parents came to help that it was finished in a day and a half!

The next week, the school musical was presented on Tuesday evening, and Mr. Baker was there to record it on videotape. On Thursday he met with the parents' group working to start a middle school program at Huntington Woods. Friday morning he came in to set up refreshments for a group of visitors, because he is a member of the Hospitality Action Team. The all-school picnic was held the next Monday, so Mr. Baker arrived at 3:00 PM to start grilling hot dogs. When the principal asked him jokingly, "Wayne, don't you think you may be a little over-involved?" he replied, "I love it here. This is like another family for me, and I feel good being here. All of you always make me feel welcome, and I know that there are so many others putting in time and effort as I do but maybe in different ways. I love it."

On a year-end feedback form for Parent Action Teams, Wayne Baker wrote this to the teacher who worked with his team:

> A year ago...when I signed up, I must admit I had no idea what action teams were or what they did, but I can't tell you what a joy it has been to be a part of such a great group of people. I can't imagine choosing a better team. You and all the other members of the team have made me feel so welcome and a part of the team...I'm sure others feel good about their action teams, but I sure am proud to be a member of the Hospitality Team! I hope I have the opportunity to work with you...for many years to come.

Our efforts to communicate effectively with parents and involve them in the school have had wonderful results. We find that the more parents understand about our goals and philosophy, and the reasons for the things we do, the more they are willing to support the school. Their attitude carries over to the children, as the students' love of Huntington Woods carries over to their parents.

CONCLUSION

Bringing the philosophy of the Quality School to life is a process of evolution and growth, unique for every set of circumstances. We emphasize that the innovations we are making at Huntington Woods are our way of implementing these ideas, and nothing described here is a prescription or recipe for other educators to follow.

We hope that our experiences will provide useful suggestions for practicing teachers and administrators, and stimulate thought and discussion among those who share our goal of quality education for all students. Other Quality Schools are being developed in many locations, and their experiences add to the body of useful ideas available. As all of us continue to learn and assess what we are doing, our schools will keep on changing and improving.

The students and parents we are serving should have the last word on Huntington Woods School. Parent Janet Rea said:

The operation of Huntington Woods is by far the best that I'm aware of for kids and for families. [Our family was] first intrigued by the year-round calendar. It extends the time for outside activities we can do with kids. In Michigan, it's pretty cold in winter, but with school into July, we have chances for picnics, working in the gardens, going on field trips. My husband and I believe there is too much lost in three-month layover.

We're really in favor of the students eating lunch in the classroom and also choice time instead of recess. We have a son who, if he's going to get into trouble, he's going to pick one of those two times. In his defense, if you put 350 kids at a gallop in a cafeteria, with maybe a worker there to supervise them, who isn't going to get in trouble then?

It's a thrill for me as a parent, first of all, to see that the kids are really learning things, and secondly, to learn with them. I've learned a whole lot more about flight than I ever thought I was going to learn when Jillian's room worked on flight recently. We went to the airport, we made airplanes, and birdhouses, and birds. It's wonderful integrated learning that is very impressive. But it doesn't happen because someone just says poof, we're going to have central study. The staff is very, very committed, and as a result, they get the parents involved right along with them.

Kaye recently talked with Danielle and Matt, who are quite new to Huntington Woods. She asked them what their other schools had been like, and to compare their experiences at Huntington so far.

Matt said, "At my other school, if people were behaving good, they got points. If you won for being the goodest, you got candy out of the goodie jar. Only one person can win in a day, and I felt bad when I didn't win. When some kids at my table were talking, we had to put our heads down on the table. I got mad because I was the only one behaving. It wasn't fair. Some of the teachers were not very nice. The art teacher slammed the door to make kids be quiet. A lot of kids got into fights there."

Danielle said, "At first I didn't want to come to Huntington Woods, because I didn't have any friends here. My Dad made me come, and 'boom,' now I'm here. Now I'm glad to be here. The kids here treat me very nice, and I have some friends now. Darren always smiles and says 'hi,' and all the boys are nice. At my old school, two particular boys were really mean to me. They twisted my arm and were always calling me names."

Matt went on, "Huntington Woods is good because people are at a Quality School and they won't steal or pick fights. I'm getting along with others here, too. Everyone in my learning family is my friend already.

Danielle put in, "The teachers here are fun, and I like the work we do. I am learning a lot of new science and everything. The teachers here don't yell at us. They just explain it so we understand. I like the computer lab, too. At the computer lab at my old school, we didn't have very many computers, and the kids fought over them.

Matt said, "My mom and dad like this school because we help the poor at Casey's. I like Job Corps because I get to clean things, and I'm good at that. I really, really like choice time. I've enjoyed music. We do a lot of cool stuff here—art, music, games, all the activities we get to do. I like eating lunch in the classrooms. The teachers here are nice, and the principal. It already feels like I've known Mrs. V my whole life."

214

REFERENCES and RESOURCES

Works listed here include those cited in the text and other resources that readers might find helpful.

Books and articles

Anderson, J. *50 Strategies for Quality Teaching: A handbook for the Application of Control Theory in classroom settings.* Minneapolis: Jackpine Publishing, 1995. Available from publisher at PO Box 80711, Minneapolis, MN 55408.

Anderson, R.H. and B.N. Pavan. *Nongradedness: Helping It to Happen.* Lancaster, PA: Technomic Publishing Company, 1993.

Armstrong, Thomas. *The Myth of the ADD Child: 50 Ways to Improve Your Child's Behavior and Attention Span Without Drugs, Labels, or Coercion.* New York: Dutton division of Penguin Books, 1995.

_____*Seven Kinds of Smart: Identifying and Developing Your Many Intelligences.* New York: Plume/Penguin, 1993.

Ben Ari, R., and Y. Rich. *Meeting the Educational Needs of All Students in the Heterogenous Class.* In *To Be Young and Gifted*, P.S. Klein and A.J. Tannenbaum, Editors. Norwood, NJ: Ablex Publishing, 1992.

Berman, Sally. *A Multiple Intelligences Road to a Quality Classroom.* Palatine: IRI/Skylight Training and Publishing, 1995.

Bonstingl, J.J. *The Total Quality Classroom.* In *Educational Leadership* 49: 6 (1992), pp. 71-75.

Greaves, N. and T., Eds, *Cooperative Learning.* Write for subscriptions or back issues to editors Drs. Nancy and Ted Graves, IASCE, Box 1582, Santa Cruz, CA 95061-1582. (408) 426-7926.

Crawford, D., R. Bodine, and R. Hoglund. *The School for Quality Learning: Managing the School and Classroom the Deming Way.* Champaign: Research Press, 1994.

Deming, W.E. *Out of Crisis*. Cambridge, MA: MIT. (1986)

Dunn, R., K. Dunn & J. Perrin. *Teaching Young Children Through Their Individual Learning Styles: Practical Approaches for Grades K-2.* Boston: Allyn and Bacon, 1994.

Edison Project. *Partnership School Design.* The Edison Project, 1994. Contact publisher at 529 Fifth Avenue, 122th Floor, New York, NY 10017, fax (212) 309-1604.

Educational Leadership. M.M. Scherer, Ed. Journal of the Association for Supervision and Curriculum Development. 1250 N. Pitt St., Alexandria, VA 22314-1453.

Educators in Connecticut Pomperaug Regional School District 15. *A Teacher's Guide to Performance-based Learning and Assessment.* Alexandria, VA: Association for Supervision and Curriculum Development, 1996.

Floyd, Carleen. *My Quality World Workbook.* Waterloo: TSM Leadership Associates, 1990.

Gardner, Howard. *Multiple Intelligences: The Theory In Practice.* NY: BasicBooks, A Division of HarperCollins Publishers, Inc., 1993.

The Unschooled Mind: How Children Think and How Schools Should Teach. NY: BasicBooks, Division of HarperCollins Publishers, Inc., 1991.

Gaustad, Joan. *Nongraded Education: Mixed-age, Integrated, and Developmentally Appropriate Education for Primary Children.* OSSC Bulletin 35:7 (1992). Oregon School Study Council, Stuart C. Smith, Ed.

Glasser, William. *Choice Theory: A New Psychology of Personal Freedom.* New York: HarperCollins, forthcoming in 1997.

_____ Unpublished lecture, Cincinnati, Ohio, 1997.

_____ Unpublished lecture. Minneapolis, 1996.

_____ *The Control Theory Manager.* New York: HarperCollins, 1994.

_____ *The Quality School Teacher.* New York: HarperCollins, 1993.

_____ *The Quality School.* New York: Harper & Row, 1990.

_____ *Control Theory in the Classroom.* New York: Harper & Row, 1986.

_____ *Control Theory.* New York: Harper & Row, 1984.

_____ *Schools Without Failure,* First Edition. New York: Harper & Row, 1969.

_____ *Reality Therapy.* New York: Harper & Row, 1965.

Goleman, Daniel. *Social and Emotional Intelligence.* NY: Bantam Books, 1995.

Good, E.P. *Overall Direction: A Guide to Getting Where You Want to Go and Being Who You Want to Be.* Chapel Hill, NC: New View Publications, 1996.

Goodlad, J. I. and R. H. Anderson. *The Nongraded Elementary School.* New York: Teachers College Press, 1987.

Greene, Bradley H. *New Paradigms for Quality Schools.* Chapel Hill, NC: New View Publications, 1996.

_____ *Self Esteem and the Quality School.* Simi Valley: Self Esteem and the Quality School, an Educational Consulting Firm, 1989. Available from Brad Greene, 938 Rivera Street, Simi Valley, CA 93065. (805) 527-5291.

Haggerty, Brian A. *Nurturing Intelligence: A Guide to Multiple Intelligences Theory and Teaching.* NY: Addison Wesley, 1995.

Hocutt, Anne M. *Effectiveness of Special Education: Is Placement the Critical Factor?* in *The Future of Children*, Richard E. Behrman, Ed.,Vol. 6 No. 1 (Spring 1996), Center for the Future of Children, David and Lucille Packard Foundation.

Inclusion Times. Newsletter available form National Professional Resources, Inc., 25 So. Regent Street, Port Chester, NY.

Jensen, Eric. *Brain-Based Learning and Teaching.* Del Mar, CA: Turning Point Publishing, 1995. Contact publisher at Box 2551, Del Mar, CA 92014. Phone 619-755-6670; fax 619-792-2858.

Johnson, David W. and others. *Circles of Learning.* Revised version, 1986. Available from Interaction Book Co., 7208 Cornelia Drive, Edina, Minnesota 55435.

Johnson, David and Roger, *Cooperation and Competition.* Edina, MN: Interaction Book Company, 1989.

Jonsson, Cheryl. *Reflections on Portfolios.* Reprinted in *The William Glasser Institute Newsletter*, summer, 1996. Chatsworth: The William Glasser Institute. Write for information, 22024 Lassen Street #118, Chatsworth, CA 91311. Fax (818) 700-0555.

Karrass, Chester L. and W. Glasser. *Both-Win Management.* New York: Lippincott and Crowell, 1980.

Katz, L. *The Case for Mixed-age Grouping in Early Education.* Washington, DC: National Association for the Education of Young Children, 1990.

Kohn, Alfie. Punished By Rewards: The Trouble With Gold Stars, Incentive Plans, A's, Praise, and Other Bribes. Boston: Houghton-Mifflin, 1993.

Lazear, David. *Seven Ways of Knowing: Understanding Multiple Intelligences*, second edition. Palatine, IL: Skylight Publishing, Inc., 1991.

Lickona, Thomas. *Educating for Character: How Our Schools Can Teach Respect and Responsibility.* New York: Bantam Books, 1991.

Mamary, Al. *Ten Guidelines for Maximum Inclusion of Special Needs Students.* In *Journal for Quality Learning*, F. McDowell, Sr., Ed. 6:2 (1996), p.39. Bear, DE: Partners for Quality Learning. To subscribe, contact Partners for Quality Learning, 11 Dover Court, Porter Square, Bear, DE 19701.

Marzano, Robert J. *A Different Kind of Classroom: Teaching with Dimensions of Learning.* Alexandria, VA: Association for Supervision and Curriculum Development, 1250 N. Pitt St., Alexandria, VA 22314. 1992.

Mentley, K. *Quality Tips.* In *Quality Connections* 1:1, September, 1997. K. Mentley and S. Ludwig, Eds., To subscribe, contact KWM Educational Services, 4967 Chableau Dr., SW, Wyoming, MI 49509. Fax (616) 534-1457.

The New City School. *Celebrating Multiple Intelligences: Teaching for Success.* St. Louis, MO: The New City School, Inc., 1994.

Pavan, B.N. The Benefits of Nongraded Schools *Educational Leadership* 50:2. 1992, pp 22-25.

_____*The Nongraded Elementary School: Research on Academic Achievement and Mental Health.* in *Texas Tech Journal of Education,* 4 (1977), Pp. 91-107.

Rekkas, Alexandria. *Strategies for Inclusion: An Annotated Bibliography.* In *Childhood Education: Journal of the Association for Childhood Education International,* Pp. 168-171. 11501 Georgia Ave, suite 315, Wheaton, MD 20902. Fax (301) 942-3012.

Rhoades, Jacqueline and Margaret E. McCabe. *The Cooperative Classroom: Social and Academic Activities.* Bloomington, IN: National Educational Service, 1992.

Richarz, S. *Innovations In Early Childhood Education: Models that Support the Integration of Children of Varied Developmental Levels.* In *Integrating young children with disabilities into community programs,* C. Peck, S. Odom & D. Bricker, Eds. Baltimore, MD: Paul H. Brookes 1993.

Schatz, Anne, and Ronda Pifer. *School Reform and Restructuring Through the Use of the "Quality School" Philosophy*. Journal of Quality Learning, F. McDowell, Sr., Ed., 6:2 (1996).

Slavin, Robert E. *Cooperative Learning: Theory, Research, and Practice.* Englewood Cliffs, NJ: Prentice Hall, 1990.

Tinsley, Mariwyn and Mona G. Perdue. *The Journey to Quality:Translating the Quality School Concepts Into Action in your Staffroom and Classroom.* Chapel Hill, NC: New View Publications, 1992.

Van der Laan, Andrea. *Self Evaluation and Change Are Not Dirty Words.* Unpublished article, 1997.

Vincent, Philip F. *Developing Character in Students: A Primer.* Chapel Hill, NC: New View Publications, 1994.

Wubbolding, Robert E. *Reality Therapy With Children.* In Kratochwill and Morris, Eds., *Psychotherapy With Children and Adolescents.* Allyn & Bacon, 1993.

_____*Understanding Reality Therapy.* New York: HarperCollins, 1991.

_____ *Using Reality Therapy.* New York: HarperCollins, 1988.

Videotapes

Armstrong, Thomas. *The Myth of the ADD Child.* (1995). Videotape available from National Professional Resources, Inc., 25 South Regent St., Port Chester, NY 19573. Tel: 1-800-453-7461, Fax: (914) 937-9327.

Building a Quality School: A Matter of Responsibility. Teacher's version, Administrator's version. Videotape available from National Professional Resources, Inc., Department VJ.

Dr. William Glasser. Videotape available from National School Conference Institute.

Internet resources

The William Glasser Institute: http//wglasserinst.com

Quality Schools Forum: http//QualitySchools.com

Contact Huntington Woods Elementary School:

Kaye Mentley, Principal
4330 Byron Center Avenue, SW
Wyoming, Michigan 49509

Fax: (616) 249-7656
Telephone: (616) 530-7537

Acknowledgements

We are grateful to the Huntington Woods Elementary School family of students, parents, teachers, and staff members who in their daily lives and work help make the Quality School a reality. You are the people who will carry these ideas for the coming generation. We respect your integrity, caring, and intelligence, and we love you very much.

We also have great respect for Richard Carlson, Superintendent, Anita Rutlin, Deputy Superintendent, Lee Pierce, Assistant Superintendent, and the Wyoming Public School Board of Education for their professional courage and continuing support of Huntington Woods.

Many people helped make this book possible by giving generously of their thoughts, time, energy, written words, friendship, and support. Thank you, family members Marc Mentley, Chris Mills, and Alison Mills. From the very beginning our close friend Jeanette McDaniel helped create and shape the ideas for this book. Thanks also to the friends, mentors, and colleagues who helped and encouraged us in so many ways: Dr. Robert Wubbolding, Sandra Wubbolding, Linda Harshman, Carmen Hannah, Brad Greene, Robert Hansen, Patricia Darley, Sally Fleming, Lynda Golletz, Brigitte Harris, Keith Myles, and Janice Pettis. You add quality to our lives!

The authors publish *Quality Connections*, a bulletin of useful Quality School ideas for practicing teachers and administrators. Each issue focuses on a theme, and is filled with tips, energizer and involvement activities, 'food for thought,' questions and answers, and resource information. We invite you to request a complimentary sample issue.

Book and Subscription Order Form

Quality Connections: Published eight times during the school year, from September to May. Subscribing at any time will bring you eight issues, beginning with the current one.

_____ Please send a free issue of *Quality Connections*.

_____ One-year subscription (8 issues) for $48 U.S., $51 U.S. to international addresses.

Quality Is the Key: Stories from Huntington Woods School

_____ copies of the book at $14 U.S. each, plus shipping ($2 for the first book $1 for each additional).
_____Amount enclosed

Name_____

Address_____

City_____

State, Province, Zip Code_____

Country_____

Fax purchase orders: (616) 534-1457   **School/company**
Postal orders: KWM Educational Services   **Purchase Orders**
           4967 Chableau Drive, SW   **accepted**
           Wyoming, Michigan 49509